"This compassionate book provides specific tools for successful personal empowerment—highly recommended for anyone who overeats or has obsessed about weight loss."

Leigh Cohn,
MAT, CEDS, coauthor of *Self-Esteem Tools for Recovery*

•

"Finally, the best non-diet 'diet' book I've read."

Jan Patenaude,
Registered Dietitian

•

" . . . an incredible empowerment tool that shows how to become responsible in life and take control of your destiny."

Lisa Ford,
author of *Become a Conscious Creator: A Return to Self-Empowerment*

•

"*Body Redesign: Goal Setting Secrets for a Thinner, Happier You* provides a step-by-step guide to integrating emotional healing with real behavioral change. Dr. Colby guides the reader through a journey of self-awareness and forgiveness to find the way to true healing."

Joannah Ginsburg,
LMSW, therapist—Lifeworks Counseling, Dallas, Texas

"I am loving the book and can't put it down! Dr. Colby really knows what to write to capture the real meaning behind overeating. Absolutely fantastic!"

Laura Economos,
founder of Nutrizone Total Body Nourishment, Sydney, Australia

•

"As a person who highlights for importance and emphasis, I find every line to be worthy of highlighting. This is a remarkable workbook!"

Susan Glidewell,
eating disorder technician

•

"A truly uplifting guide written with great care! Dr. Colby gently carves out a path for the reader to take courageous steps toward self-change, self-love, and the realization that life's fullness is indeed a gift for all to enjoy.

Elise A. Oberliesen,
freelance writer, Westminster, Colorado

•

"*Goal Setting Secrets for a Thinner, Happier You* changed my life! It showed me how to define my dreams and how to take action to turn those dreams into reality."

Adrienne Cocita,
Plano, Texas

BODY REDESIGN

Goal Setting Secrets for a Thinner, Happier You

For Becky Johnson —

All the best,
and lots of joy!

Annette Colby

For Becky Johnson –

All the best,
And lots of joy!

[signature]

BODY REDESIGN

Goal Setting Secrets for a Thinner, Happier You

Annette Colby, PhD, RD

BROWN BOOKS   DALLAS, TEXAS

BODY REDESIGN
Goal Setting Secrets for a Thinner, Happier You

Manufactured in the United States of America

For information, please contact:

Brown Books Publishing Group
16200 North Dallas Parkway, Suite 170
Dallas, Texas 75248
www.brownbooks.com
972-381-0009

A New Era in Publishing™

ISBN-13: 978-1-934812-07-5
ISBN-10: 1-934812-07-2
LCCN 2007943661

1 2 3 4 5 6 7 8 9 10

This publication is designed to provide accurate and authoritative information concerning the subject matter covered. It is sold with the understanding that the publisher is not engaged in rendering psychological, financial, legal, or other professional services. If expert assistance or counselling is needed, the services of a competent professional should be sought.

To my husband

Ray Nowicki

⊸⊙ Always & Forever ⊙⊶

Contents

List of Goal Worksheets

You can download printable forms at www.AnnetteColby.com/goalforms

And did you get what
you wanted from this life even so?

I did.

And what did you want?

To call myself beloved, to feel myself
beloved on the earth.

—Raymond Carver, American Writer—

The Good Life

Acknowledgments

Thank you to my friends and family who have let me know all along that I am loved and appreciated. Thank you to Siegfried Klomann and Renate Klomann; to Dad, for his unfolding warmth and compassion; and to Mom, for sharing her love of passionate cooking and her strength of determination.

Thank you to my publisher, Milli Brown, for her generosity of spirit and to the staff at Brown Books Publishing Group for treating my work with such respect.

Thank you to the inspirational women in my life, including Francie White, V. Jan Marszalek, Ann Weiser Cornell, and Karin Kratina, who each in their own ways helped give birth to this book.

Finally, my deepest gratitude to my growing family of readers who inspire me to continue writing.

Introduction

—Goals: When "Just Do It" Doesn't Work—

Ending your struggle with food and weight is not just a matter of motivation. If you are like many people battling with food issues, you are very motivated and perhaps even desperate to lose weight. Through your efforts, you have probably already learned how to eat "right" and how to "behave" in order to lose weight. You know the "rules" of nutrition and exercise. You have most likely lost weight numerous times. However, to achieve the complete fulfillment of your dreams, you need skills and tools beyond motivation. You also need precise techniques that provide a dynamic alternative to willpower when "just do it" is not enough.

If you are reading this book, you are ready to create a life that does not revolve around eating, dieting, or obsessing about food. You are at the place in your personal journey where you want to rise above struggling with issues of food and body weight. You are ready to move beyond the lure of diets or prescribed plans and take matters more fully into your own hands. This entails empowering yourself with new skills, deciding for yourself what a more meaningful life would encompass, and then acting to achieve that. This means going beyond expecting or hoping that someone else will fix your life. It means going a step further than knowing that you do not want to eat a certain way, and instead choosing for yourself the life experiences you would rather have.

Making peace with food and reclaiming your life is a journey. It involves stepping out of habitual ways of dealing with life and stepping into a new awareness of alternative possibilities. The aim of this book is to help you create new routines, release old assumptions, and become sensitive to what you really want for yourself. Learning the skills contained within these pages can help you break out of the patterns of self-destruction and choose to live life in a new way. Read the following list and highlight the experiences and behaviors common to you:

- Do you feel powerless when it comes to food?

- Do you eat when you are not hungry?

- Do you eat large quantities of food at one time?

- Do you eat to run away from your feelings?

- Do you eat to create the illusion of feeling good?

- Do you feel guilty after you eat?

- Does your weight affect the way you live?

- Do you eat to escape from stress, worries, or boredom?

- Do you eat differently in private than you do in public?

- Do you think about food constantly?

- Do you eat until you are uncomfortably full?

- Do you continually attempt one diet or food plan after another, with no lasting success?

- Do you spend a lot of time thinking about food and how to acquire it?

- Do you eat in secret or hide food?

- Do you eat when you feel empty inside?

- Do you feel fearful of a future that is out of control?

Life feels good when you take charge of deciding what you want, particularly when you take the steps to accomplish it. This does not mean pushing at goals or pushing at your self. On the contrary, it means deciding what you want, becoming excited about the possibility of it becoming reality, and using a combination of heart, spirit, and logic to create motivation for action.

I wrote this book because I understand that none of us can alter the course of our lives if we do not understand the steps involved in how to create a new future. We have to know how to develop a well-designed goal and unleash inner motivation—from start to finish—before we can move beyond our current ways of living and acting. *Body Redesign: Goal Setting Secrets for a Thinner, Happier You* provides the processes and techniques needed to help you develop a clear and steady plan and then take the small gradual steps needed to achieve your goals.

Having what you want is important. In fact, there is nothing more important in your life than moving your desires to the top of your priority list. By following the steps outlined, you uncover the miracle of knowing that you can raise your confidence, feel happy in the body you were born with, and achieve your desires. My goal is to teach valuable techniques and provide the tools to help you overcome your fears and obstacles, and help you develop greater self-leadership so that you can attain your dreams. My aim is to help you take control of how your life evolves. As you read this book and work through the various exercises, may a growing sense of inspiration and love open within you. May you hear a new voice that says, "I can reinvent my life and move through this 'impossible' situation." What I can teach you will enable you to move through the barriers that block your happiness. To reach this objective, you will learn to:

- look beyond the problem and instead develop crystal-clear future expectations

- gain a sense of control about your life and your future

- face your excuses and end them

- remain positively focused on solutions and opportunities

- commit to the life you want to live

- remain focused on top priorities, concentrating on what is most important and rewarding

- love yourself like you have never been loved before . . . by giving yourself what you most want!

The rewards of creating change are great. As you move through the process of transforming your world, you will uncover lightness and love you did not know you had. You will experience a level of freedom you did not know was possible. However, there is a catch. To find your happiness, your purpose, and live a different life requires exploring unfamiliar territory. Quite often, newness is frightening and uncomfortable. You open yourself to new challenges. Painful beliefs will surface and make themselves apparent in your thoughts and emotions. You will find yourself facing the need to take risks and make unfamiliar decisions. The entire process of creating a new future is really an adventure in which you invite yourself to discover if you can become more than you currently believe yourself capable of becoming.

Goal setting is not only about lifting your self out of one undesired reality but also about relying on yourself to imagine and then generate a new, more desirable reality. Compassionate, yet strong, self-leadership is required throughout this life transition. Goals, when approached correctly, take you systematically through a process that allows you to gain the necessary skills, self-love, power, and balance needed to exit out of an old reality and enter into a new life. The process—including all of your challenges, setbacks, and failures—is required to release your disempowerment beliefs and step into your life as a self-loving, self-ruling person.

Setting and achieving goals allows you to recover autonomy and take control of your life. Instead of pushing down emotions, you learn the value of intense feelings.

Although uncomfortable, strong emotions possess the wisdom of exactly what is wrong in your life, what you currently believe about yourself and your abilities, and what inner strengths you need to develop to live a better life. This wisdom, if used properly, can be the key that sets you free.

Building success around food and your weight requires an entirely different way of believing, thinking, and acting. Setting goals shows you how to take responsibility for your life, attain new self-empowering skills, and achieve success. Your goal setting and achieving process is not so much about the final victory, although that will come, as it is about utilizing each new challenge as an opportunity to strengthen your capacity to make life-enhancing decisions. You learn to choose a meaningful life-direction and concentrate your efforts on something that is important to you. As you make your needs a priority, your self-esteem rises. As you take self-loving action, you reclaim personal power. Recognizing achievements along the way, you realize you do indeed have the power to effect change in your life. Goals initiate a new balance between logic and creative spirit, allowing you to feel more complete, more fulfilled, and happier than you have ever felt.

This plan is designed to show you the simplest way to create the rich and rewarding life you desire. However, this book will be of little value if you only read the words. I suggest that you systematically and actively engage yourself in the completion of each of the exercises and worksheets. The point of the exercises is to provide a template to reveal *what* the tools of success are, why each tool is important, and simultaneously to provide you with an *experiential opportunity* to practice using those tools. At first, it may seem awkward and time-consuming to fill out these forms. You may shy away from the exercises, believing them too cumbersome. You are right—learning any new skill feels uncomfortable, and you may not initially see the value of following the system in the way it is presented. Deciding to follow the exercises is an act of faith, as you risk attempting new behaviors while not yet knowing if those behaviors will succeed. Allow me to reassure you that you will benefit by involving yourself in the process.

This workbook provides a specific action plan to end emotional eating, compulsive eating, binge eating, secret eating, or bulimic behaviors. Yet, it is so much more than that! Once you have learned to apply the concepts provided in this plan to achieve your desired eating or weight goal, you can easily apply these same principles to other areas of your life. You will grasp how wonderful it is that you now have the ability to control other areas of your life. You will be in the driver's seat as you decide for yourself what direction you will head, how to get there, and when you will arrive.

After you have worked through the plan for yourself, the basics will be part of your new vocabulary and thought process. You will know how to uncover your dreams, passions, and desires and then make them happen. Having obtained the fundamentals, you will be free to experiment with these tools in your own creative way. Have fun with them, redesign them, and make them yours. In due course, as you master the concepts, you can move into a life beyond goal setting.

Ultimately, life is not really about systematically setting goal after goal. It is, however, a continuous process of freeing yourself from your own self-imposed limitations, discovering where you wish to direct your efforts and life-energy, and bringing new dreams into this reality. Setting goals, as described in this book, teaches you how to do that. Take the time and learn the fundamentals. Begin with the proven principles of success, apply them to your own life, and *then* be free to create your own system of success. For now, take a deep breath and fill your entire body with the recognition that you are at an amazing place in your personal journey! You are about to leave your old ways behind and lead yourself into a more fulfilling and meaningful life. You are ready to take the next steps of your journey.

Twelve Skills to Reclaim Your Life

The process of building a new future is an interesting undertaking. In order to succeed you must have the knowledge, skills, and supportive attitudes necessary to adopt and maintain your desired change. Even when you know what to do, it is often difficult to get yourself to take consistent action. It is just not that easy to get up and do something different. A lifetime of ingrained habits, feelings of hopelessness, and so many other obstacles stand in the way of a happier, healthier life.

Body Redesign: Goal Setting Secrets for a Thinner, Happier You offers a blend of science and heart to help you overcome obstacles, develop balance, deepen your love of self, and attain the life you want to live. This book provides a systematic method to help you overcome feeling stuck, end overeating, and build a more joyful life. Each page lists new ideas of exactly how to move forward and change your life in a positive way. Listed below is a synopsis and overview of the twelve core skills contained in this book that allow you to build your goals from the ground up, permeate those goals with inspiration, and transform your desires into real life.

Skill One—You Can't Win the War Against Yourself

If you have picked up this book, it is because you are realizing that battling your weight or being at war with yourself has not provided the solution you had anticipated. Goals deliver a system in which you not only call a truce with your self, body, and food, they also show you how to structure a brand new life. You are no longer spending your energy trying to win a battle. Instead, you open the doorway to new possibilities. You may discover that your eating challenge was a blessing in disguise as it leads you to take your future into your own hands. Your wish to end certain eating behaviors represents your desire to create peace within and feel better. This does not happen through battle or struggle. It happens when you make new choices about how you live your life and how you treat your human self. By setting forth on a journey with a specific direction and a clear plan, you dare to discover that, despite your current challenges and unhappiness, you are capable of making new things happen. As you make new decisions about your future and discover how to move forward, you will receive irrefutable proof that you can indeed have exactly what you want in life. You can live a life of your choosing and attain that life without battle.

Skill Two—Benefits Must Outweigh Costs

At some point in your life you began using food to cope with a painful living situation, a difficult life experience, an unresolved inner conflict, or emotional suppression. In response to ongoing frustration, stress, boredom, disappointment, or feeling that your life was out of control, you began using food as an unconscious means to feel better. Food provided a readily accessible answer and offered a sense of calm, distraction, or emotional numbness. Your initial decision to turn to food was a self-loving choice, at the time, as you found a way of temporarily making yourself feel better. Now, however, you are ready to move forward in your life and discover new ways of living. To achieve this objective you cannot just end your eating behaviors. The cost of removing your way of surviving life would be too high. Instead, you must fill your needs with new, more life-enhancing strategies. These strategies include creating a shift in how you see the world and your place in it and replacing the function that food once served with compassion, stability, and greater confidence.

Skill Three—Identify Your Underlying Motivations

To sustain lasting, long-term motivation you must know your underlying motivations for wanting to change. Certainly, you want to change your eating behaviors or lose weight, but you want more than that. You want to feel or experience the tangible benefits of your goal on a day-to-day basis. Your compelling reasons are the answers to why you want to stop your eating behaviors or lose weight. What inner strengths, talents, or personality traits will you unearth? What fear do you want to release or move past? These underlying or compelling reasons are about defining what you value in life and then using those values to guide your journey. It is a definition of who you are, what you stand for, and what is important to you. Knowing your underlying motivation helps keep you focused on your priorities in life and the goals you have for yourself. It gives you a chance to start over and make different choices. It gives you clear direction, and you are less likely to take the easy way out or accept short-term gains at the expense of your long-term goals. You make good decisions and quickly know which choices support you and which do not. You live with integrity, become a whole person, and live with choices that allow you to be true to your self. It is time to go beneath the surface reasons of your goal and discover the real reasons for why you are about to embark on this life-changing journey.

Skill Four—Illuminate Your Ideal Future

Before you can live a happier and improved life, you have to know what it is that you want, and you have to be able to articulate that vision. Without the ability to choose your big picture of long-term desires—no matter how badly you want to improve your life or how hard you wish for it—you will not be able to create that experience for yourself. You must learn a simple system to develop and express crystal-clear future expectations. First, utilize your natural ability to grumble and complain and allow your dissatisfactions to work for you. Once you identify your areas of discontent, the reverse of these experiences or feelings often reveals a clear picture of what you want to have for your life. Being able to set a big-picture goal gives you something solid to believe in, to spend your energy and efforts on, and to guide your decisions. Once your big-picture goal is in place, it tends to be unchanging, and thereby gives you strength and direction.

Skill Five—Generate a Living, Breathing, Inspired Plan

Once you know your big-picture goal, your task involves bringing that future vision into your current reality in a way that makes your life better right now. To do so requires *inspired action*. This is a new balance between your logical abilities and your creative-inspiration abilities. Without this essential balance, you will fail to establish fulfilling, long-term success. Inspiration is the part of you that dreams wonderful outcomes. It is your ability to see a future beyond your current experience. It is also your ability to know intuitively which action is right for right now. Logic is the analytical, methodical, action-oriented aspect of self. Logic is the part of you that follows through by taking the inspired idea and turning it into a practical, today action step. Combining balanced inspiration and logic allows you to bring your future vision into today and feel better right now.

With your knowledge of balanced inspiration and logic now in place, take advantage of the science of goal setting and use the SMART system to build your goals in a specific, motivational, attainable, realistic, and time-bound manner. Instead of reinventing the wheel, learn from the wisdom of others and create a personal roadmap to success with the help of this invaluable resource.

Skill Six—Take Action

Congratulations! You have laid a solid foundation for success. Now it is time to get into the day-by-day reality of making your dreams come true. To do this requires adopting the one habit that all successful individuals possess. This single habit is the simplest but, most likely, also the most powerful lesson in this book: Take action every day. If you do nothing else but focus on the life you want to live, and then take one action step every day toward making your dreams come true, you will have taken control of your life. Taking action, even one small action every day, changes your life. It connects you to your dream, solidifies the choice you have made for yourself, and gets things moving in a new direction.

Skill Seven—Bring Your Goal into Balance

As you already know, ending overeating, emotional eating, or compulsive types of eating behaviors involves more than an "eat less, exercise more" approach. You need an action plan that includes the acquisition of new life skills. These actions allow you to take responsibility for your life, learn new skills, and become the person you want to become. Understanding that your actions and efforts will span many areas of your life can help you see beyond the immediate problem of eating and weight loss. Your focus shifts to the solution of developing a happier life by placing yourself as a priority and taking care of all your needs.

Skill Eight—Focus on Success

One of the more harmful myths of goal achieving is that it has to be motivated with willpower and harsh self-discipline. While these motivational strategies may work over the short-term, you are only likely to succeed over the long-term if you focus on what is working and keep adjusting your actions so that you continue to feel successful. Success generates more success. Along each and every step of the way take credit for your actions. Delight in your efforts and accomplishments. Every day, take a few minutes to list all your attempts at improvement. Do not merely highlight the successes, but stress each endeavor. No matter how minute, each undertaking deserves recognition.

Skill Nine—Gain the Power of Personal Responsibility

Personal responsibility is the ability to accept that whether or not you are responsible for your situation, you decide to act as though you are because it gives you the power to choose differently. The acceptance of personal responsibility is what lifts you out of the muck and stagnancy of your life. Your decision to take action, even when faced with an almost overwhelming desire not to, releases inner power. Personal responsibility is your key to freedom. It is your path to creating a healthy self-to-self relationship, in which you act as a self-caring individual. You have the ability to turn your life around and reclaim your power. However, the only way to retrieve your power is to face inner resistance and move forward anyway. Doing this is difficult beyond description. It will feel impossible, unfair, and emotional. Yet, once you move beyond your inertia and accept personal responsibility for the outcome of your life, you will taste the delicious freedom of your own power. Personal responsibility involves asking yourself: Will you support you in your desire to live differently, even when times get tough? Will you do what it takes to give yourself what you most want?

Skill Ten—Face Your Excuses and End Them

When you set your goal, you commit to love and cherish it. You agree to show up and take action. There is an unspoken agreement to be fully devoted to the relationship between you and your desire. However, many of us make promises and commitments to ourselves that we fully intend to keep—*if* nothing else gets in the way or if the task does not involve discomfort. Generally, when the going gets tough, we find excuses of why we cannot take action or move forward. These excuses are the lies we tell to ourselves and allow ourselves to believe as truth. However, if we are willing to take a closer look at our excuses, we will see that there is always a creative solution to any obstacle. Challenges, obstacles, and the resulting excuses are expected and unavoidable. Your goal will involve discomfort. The important point is what will you do when your excuses appear? Will you respect yourself and honestly work through the conflict? Alternately, will you buy into your own excuses without confronting yourself? Learn how to face your excuses and discover that nothing is more important than taking the necessary steps to get your life moving in your desired direction.

Skill Eleven—Develop Effective Self-Leadership

For most people, becoming an effective leader of their own lives is hard, daunting work. It requires transformation and learning new skills to achieve outstanding results for your self. Self-leadership is how you influence yourself to define and then take consistent, compassionate action on the dreams that are most important to you. Effective self-leadership means that you learn to bring out the best in yourself. You teach yourself how to become inspired and excited about your goals, rather than simply bossing yourself around. Strong self-leadership involves determining what you want, setting a course of inspired action, accepting personal responsibility for your actions or lack of action, following through with your promises to yourself, and applying humor, grace, and self-loving honesty to your journey. In this section, you learn how to identify and develop five self-chosen self-leadership characteristics. Discover how to make the most of these characteristics to guide yourself successfully and compassionately through unforeseen challenges.

Skill Twelve—Learn New Ways to Cope with Failure, Setbacks, and Obstacles

Discover the incredible truth about the one unavoidable and most difficult challenge of every goal journey: failure. There is no way to go through the process of achieving a goal without encountering obstacles, setbacks, and failure. This is the expected progression of learning any new skill set. Failure is the natural feedback system in learning a new task or accomplishing a goal. Furthermore, failure is the one experience that can lead you most quickly and most deeply into new reservoirs of appreciation and love for self. Failure offers you the opportunity to make choices: to give up on your goal and close your heart down or to use the experience as a stepping-stone to opening your heart further. You can view failure as evidence of your inherent internal flaws, or you can look within to find emotional and spiritual strengths to gain confidence and begin again.

Twelve Skill's to Success

1. You Can't Win the War Against Yourself

2. Benefits Must Outweigh Costs

3. Identify Your Underlying Motivations

4. Illuminate Your Ideal Future

5. Generate a Living, Breathing, Inspired Plan

6. Take Action

7. Bring Your Goal into Balance

8. Focus on Success

9. Gain the Power of Personal Responsibility

10. Face Your Excuses and End Them

11. Develop Effective Self-Leadership

12. Learn New Ways to Cope with Failures, Setbacks, and Obstacles

Chapter One

The Miracle of the Goal

——You Can't Win the War Against Yourself——

Let us start with an important basic question: why set goals? Why spend time reading this guide, thinking about your goals, and then writing them down? It is not as if you have not set a goal before, felt excited, started some action, and then dropped it because you quickly became overwhelmed, frustrated, or bored with the process. So, why bother this time?

The fact is that goal setting changes your life forever! Goal setting leads to the unfolding evolution of who you want to be, what you want to do, and the life you deserve to live. Setting goals is a powerful thing to do because you create an opportunity to sort out what is important from what is irrelevant in your life. It is an opportunity to give yourself a specific direction and give your energy a precise focus. It becomes easier to prioritize your time and say "no" to certain requests when you know what you want to spend your time doing. Overall, the process of setting and achieving goals leads you into a new maturity that allows you to live a more fulfilling and happier life.

So, why has it failed in the past? It is not that you are unmotivated or that setting goals is overly difficult. It is simply that most of us have only learned a portion of what we need to know about goal setting. No one has shared with us the entire process in a way that was easy to master and apply. Without the missing elements of goal setting, you will work hard and have the best of intentions but continuously struggle in your efforts to create the life you want live.

You may be saying that you hate your challenges, that you despise your body, or perhaps that you must battle your food challenges. However, if you have picked up this book, it is because you are realizing that fighting with yourself has not provided the solution you had anticipated. When you are in a war with your self it is you versus you. One part of you battles another part of you. Since both parts are you, one side may temporarily win a battle, but soon enough the other side will gather strength and win the next battle. Your energy or strength is merely shifted from one side to another, resulting in a perpetual inner tug-of-war. In this continuous battle there can be no ultimate winner and no inner peace.

Goals deliver a system in which you call a truce with your self, body, and food, and then structure a brand new life. You are no longer trying to win a battle. Instead, you open the doorway for new possibilities. Yes, it can be difficult to learn how to trust your body once again. It can be challenging to create a harmonious existence with your life. However, this is your journey and the journey of all human beings. We each learn how to gain increasing respect for our unique selves and bring our distinctive dreams into physical existence. Overcoming your challenge with food puts you into direct contact with your inner desire to create a happy, harmonious, and peaceful life. Peacefulness does not mean you sit around meditating all day. It means that you have learned how to connect with your inner dreams and apply your life energy to make them real.

Whether you engage in compulsive eating, binge eating, emotional eating, or bulimic behaviors, your overeating stems from a feeling of disempowerment in one of these five ways:

1. Believing yourself to be helpless in dealing with intense emotions.

2. Believing yourself unable to affect change in your personal life.

3. Believing that happiness comes from the external.

4. Believing yourself unable to connect with your inspiration, creativity, love, and joy.

5. Believing that it is not your place to assert your independence and individuality.

Implementing the proven methods provided in this book will lead you through these deeply ingrained beliefs and challenging emotions into empowerment and success. You can make decisions to replace these narrow concepts about yourself with new beliefs about your worth and ability to have what you want. You can stop being self-destructive and realize your creative potential.

Your eating challenge opens the doorway for new potentials and possibilities. Amazingly, you may discover that your problem was a blessing in disguise as it leads you to take your future into your own hands. Your wish to end certain eating behaviors represents your desire to feel safe and secure in your body, to create peace within, and feel better in life. This does not happen through battle or struggle. It happens when you make new choices about how you live your life and treat your human self.

By setting forth on a journey with a specific direction and a clear plan, you dare to discover that despite your current challenges and unhappiness, you are capable of making new things happen. Rather than beating yourself up during this journey, instead of being hard on yourself, your mission is an attempt to uncover a little more love of self, a little more empowerment, and a little more happiness each day. As you apply new skills and move forward with self-respect, you will receive irrefutable proof that you can indeed have exactly what you want in life.

Goal setting is an ability that will change you forever. When you learn the complete bottom-up approach of goal building, you will gift yourself with the fundamentals of success. By following the process outlined in this book you can feel happy about choosing a new direction, have motivation that lasts throughout the entire day, and feel fulfilled knowing that you are involved in bringing your dreams into reality. This time—instead of plunging directly into your desire to end overeating and lose weight or embarking on yet another diet—allow yourself to master the secrets to lifelong success and happiness.

When it comes to living a healthy and confident life, real goal achievement involves much more than good intentions. It is not enough to know you want to eat differently or that you want to lose weight. It is not enough to write your goal down on a sheet a paper. True success and fulfillment requires solid planning. Taking time to focus on the initial preparatory work may initially seem unimportant, but setting a strong foundation ensures your ability to move through the inevitable challenges and frustrations of your journey. It allows sustained motivation and anticipation about the future. Having this foundation allows you to tap back into renewed drive and motivation when you need it most.

Setting a foundation may initially seem as dull as having to buy a new set of tires for your car. Tires are plain, sort of boring, and no one notices that you just spent over five hundred dollars. Most likely, you would have rather spent the money on something more fun. However, without tires you are not going to get very far. The same is true with spending effort to set a new foundation. While you might rather skip the ground-laying steps, without a new foundation your adventure is not likely to reach your anticipated outcome. Laying out a road map for what you want allows your journey to unfold in a manner that leads to achieving real, lasting change with increased life-energy, sustained passionate focus, loving self-discipline, and positive motivation.

Part of setting a solid foundation includes taking time up front to uncover your motivating reason. While the idea of living a better life sounds wonderful in theory, the reality is that the work involved in creating change is full of effort. Although you say you want change, there are also aspects of you that do not want change. One side of you may make a decision to eat differently while another side of you may object. To move through this internal struggle you need to be able to come back to your foundation and remember the deep reasons why your journey was important. Having a strong foundation to stand on allows you to pass quickly and efficiently through the inner conflict and outer challenges. Without these basic, ground-level, fundamental pieces in place, you will face an unresolved internal power struggle and feel helpless, out of control, and frustrated. Take time to prepare your journey. Doing so will allow you to move more easily through each step of the process.

Many intelligent people wonder why they cannot just easily get a grip on their overeating. The answer comes only when they recognize that the overeating is occurring because it serves an otherwise unmet need. Ending undesirable eating habits requires so much more than just a logical solution. You cannot just stop eating, lose weight, and expect your life to be fulfilling. You cannot treat the symptoms of your problem and ignore the causes. Instead, the answer to this seemingly "easy" problem requires a complete shift in perception. Your path of creating a new future requires more than behavior change; it requires clearing away past fears and limitations. It involves adopting new beliefs that unlock inner strengths, confidence, and self-esteem. When you say you want to establish new eating habits, what you are really saying is that you want to learn the skills necessary to enter into a bigger relationship with the world, with people, and with your self. You are changing your relationship not only with food but also with life.

Consider the following life experiences:

- Having a meaningful relationship with yourself

- Feeling safe in your body and in your life

- Moving beyond your self-doubts

- Moving beyond your fears and thinking of yourself as empowered

- Embodying self-confidence and self-esteem

- Being filled with a positive attitude and self-motivated reasons for succeeding

- Being enthusiastic about life

- Implementing freedom of choice

- Taking yourself and life less seriously

- Having a sense of meaning and purpose

- Enjoying an overall sense of happiness

These are some of the experiences that all humans desire. For many of us, however, those experiences exist outside of our present reality. Goals often fail to provide the promise of a better life because many people do not consciously realize that they are not just ending a behavior. You are not only trying to become thinner. Instead, your journey of change entails the difficult task of moving beyond doubts and limitations, finding yourself worthy of creating a new self-empowered reality, and discovering how to feel better from the inside out. Goals involve the work of opening your heart more fully to yourself and life and of aligning your energy with the things you want to attain, accomplish, or achieve.

Your goal to end overeating requires you to focus on your personal values and to be the creator in your own life. Imagine . . . being the author of your own life's experiences. Imagine . . . knowing that every moment is an opportunity to reinvent your life. The words sound sweet. However, the actuality is that one must accept a huge amount of responsibility to step beyond current beliefs and life situations. New skills are necessary to venture into the conscious exploration of new life potentials and possibilities. To generate change, it is necessary to know how to tap into your spirit and move beyond beliefs stating, "I was born with this. This is my lot in life."

Setting goals allows you to assess your current circumstances, acquire self-determination, and empower yourself with confidence by saying, "I chose the actions that led to this situation, and therefore I am capable of creating a new situation." You are in charge of your life and therefore your results. You are taking responsibility to decide what kind of a person you want to be and then taking the necessary steps to line up with that self. In essence, you are asking yourself to discover if you can deliberately create something that you have never experienced. You are challenging yourself to make new decisions about your life, your strengths, your power, and your right to experience joy. Goals are the means of confronting outdated beliefs about how you feel in your body, assessing how much confidence and self-assurance you have, and making new decisions about your ability to have what you want.

If you set a goal to end your specific eating behavior, you are deciding to assume ownership for where you are and what you want. You recognize your ability to change your future and embark on an adventure to create a new relationship with your life, your body, your emotions, your thoughts, and your habits. Instead of blindly following another diet, you go on a different kind of journey to find your power and balance. You give yourself a new opportunity to challenge your current beliefs and decide if what you believe to be true must remain true. If your beliefs are not supportive of what you want, you can take action and build new beliefs that allow you to live harmoniously with your body, create a new relationship with food, handle your emotions, and feel satisfied from the inside out.

On this journey, you give up the fantasy that one day you will be rescued from your life. Without consciously realizing it, we all begin our lives with the hope that someone, anyone, outside of ourselves will give us what we so desperately need. We all dream that someone, or even a god above, will provide the magic solution that will end all of our struggles. Maybe there will be a miracle pill, an easy surgery, or someone to tell you exactly what to eat and in what proportions. Even though outside solutions may exist, believe it or not, that is not what you are seeking. There is something so much grander than being saved from your challenges. The miracle you want most is to discover that you are the very person you have been waiting for! What you desire, more than anything else, is to know that you have the power to affect change in your own life. From where you are right now, with whatever challenges you are facing, no matter how unhappy you are, you want to discover that you are capable of making new things happen.

To make new things happen you have to let go of old beliefs, attitudes, and habits. Goals allow you to move forward one step at a time and face those habitual patterns and routines. You face them so that you can choose differently. You can release your limitations and give yourself what you most want. Personal goals, like the ones involving food or weight, are different from most goals because they are all about you. They are specific areas in life where only you can give yourself the love, safety, security, confidence, or peace that you most desire. You deliberately engage in a process to affect change in your own life even as you currently believe it is impossible for you to do so.

Goals move you out of your comfort zone. They move you beyond your current beliefs and your current ways of thinking and acting. The process of change is not an easy one, and it is helpful to understand that from the beginning. It is far less frustrating when you know in advance that your goal is not simply about eating differently. Your goal is big and entails many new beliefs. The point of your goal is not whether you have an easy journey but whether you find yourself worthy of moving up your own personal ladder of evolution. The purpose of your goal is not to achieve success so that you will impress other people or receive external accolades. Quite the contrary. The miracle of your goal is that it allows you to make an amazing discovery—that you have the ability to create from the inside out and to feel good from the inside out.

At first glance, you might despise your specific eating or weight challenge; however, problems provide an impetus to tap into the strength within you! Challenges bring an awareness of feeling bad. When you have finally had enough of feeling bad, you start listening to your body and emotions, no longer ignoring the underlying message that you are not living the type of life you want to be living. This is when you begin to feel the drive to make a change. Dissatisfaction leads you to decide what a personally meaningful and happy life would look like. By setting goals, you take matters into your own hands and discover that you can end your suffering, you can increase your joy, and you are capable of creating a life that would be comfortable to you. In this way, your journey of personal evolution continues.

Along the path toward discontinuing overeating or binge eating, insight and clarity appear. Self-discovery emerges throughout the entire process, not all at once. Each discovery allows you to take the next step forward in the journey. Some of these breakthroughs include the ability to do the following:

- Decide you are worthy.

- Recognize, validate, and constructively release emotions.

- Realize that you have the ability to choose a new life direction.

- Focus thoughtful attention on desired outcomes.

- Honor your decisions by taking action.

- Increase an inner, burning desire that motivates you to your outcome.

- Love your body—even before you reach your goal.

- Connect passion and love with your dreams even before they become real.

- Increase your ability and willingness to take risks.

- Experience greater joy right now—not just after you reach success.

- Regulate how much or how little of life's abundance you receive.

- Be more aware of your purpose for being alive.

- Gain more life-energy.

- Work with your body, your emotions, and with the principles of success to create a new life.

Learning to set effective, meaningful goals provides an opportunity to gain a higher perspective of your life. You engage yourself in an active process, during which you face your fears and make new decisions. While moving forward, you must continuously decide whether to find yourself worthy, whether to forgive yourself, and whether you deserve to feel good in your life and body. A goal is not a quick fix. It is a road leading inward, and on this road, you discover self-worth and life-affecting power. During the process, you learn to stand more firmly on this earth, accepting yourself as being human, unique, sovereign, and supported. By placing attention on the dreams and goals most important to you, and by learning how to bring those goals to life, you take another step in your personal growth as you discover that you can make your life an enjoyable experience.

Unexpected Benefits of Goal Setting

When people have trouble moving beyond overeating, binge eating, or even bulimia, in part, it is because they do not understand the principles and skills required for success. If you have had enough of emotional, compulsive, binge, or overeating, get ready to take control of your life! You have the ability to create a new beginning and live a joyful, purposeful life. To whet your appetite about effective goal setting, read below and discover these unexpected benefits:

You Get to Decide Your Destiny!

How do you change your life? By accepting that you do not feel good, that you are not enjoying living in your body, and that you do not like the life experiences you are having. This wisdom ignites a tiny new flame within, a light of hope that suggests you can have more joy and success than you are currently experiencing. This light within whispers that you deserve more, that you are worthy of having more, and that your desires are important.

No matter what you tell yourself, you cannot change what is true, but. . . you can feed the light within and make something new happen. Infinite possibilities and potentials are available to you. Goals teach that you cannot continue fighting your life, your body, or your habits and expect a happy future to unfold. You have to get out of the rut and find a new path to happiness. When you set a goal, you take charge of listening to your body and making decisions. Out of all of the unlimited choices available, you decide what you intend for your life. Wow! You get to decide your destiny!

Goals Erase Feelings of Helplessness

To achieve the success you desire, you must first choose a brand-new life direction and then develop the skills and beliefs to make your dream come true. Creating the change you want is difficult because it involves confidence, certainty, and strong self-leadership skills beyond what you currently posses—at least in this area of your life. In essence, change means that you are asking yourself to be more than you believe yourself capable of being.

However, there is good news! Following the process of setting and achieving goals allows you to overcome any adversity you may meet, build the self-leadership you desire, and show you that you can live a better life. Goals bring to life the exact obstacles, struggles, and failures required to cultivate new beliefs and bring hidden strengths. As you move through the process of achieving your goal of ending overeating, you will wash away old beliefs that suggest the following:

- Things are beyond your control

- There is no point in trying because nothing ever works

- You are a victim of life

- You are helpless

- You can't have what you want

- It is not your place in the world to have more

With those beliefs intact, it is natural to look for shortcuts, magic cures, and answers outside of ourselves. However, goals allow you to challenge what you believe about yourself and your capacity to change your future. In essence, you not only wipe the slate clean, you begin again!

Goals Help You Make Peace with Your Self

Almost everyone experiences self-defeating thoughts at some point in their lives. Most of us deal with damaging patterns of self-doubt, self-criticism, and guilt in some area of life. Problems develop when these thoughts become repetitive in nature. Automatic, continuously negative thinking reinforces a distorted view that something is wrong with you. In the end, this self-criticism sabotages your success.

While your initial unhappiness with your current situation may spark awareness of your desire for change, it is love of self that allows you to move in a new direction. You want to set a new course for your life that includes motivating yourself without harsh criticism. Goals show you how to apply heart to your journey of ending food or body challenges. This new path includes compassion, honest feedback without unforgiving self-judgment, and self-respect.

Take a moment and consciously accept the physicality of your life. This means you have a body. When you hate your body, you are really saying that you hate life, that you hate being here in your life. However, when you set goals, you initiate a new potential. You accept life and decide to discover for yourself what might be possible in this land of physicality, while you are in a body, while you are alive.

To begin the process of developing a new relationship with your body, concentrate on what is right and good about you. Look at yourself as a whole person and not just a collection of mismatched or imperfect parts. Start the process of accepting your body as it is right now. For most people, accepting their current physical body is the last thing they want to consider. How can you accept what you wish to change or hate? Predictably, your immediate reaction might be an adamant objection. You probably do not want to accept your body as it is right now. However, the way your body is right now is your current reality. There is no escape from reality; in fact, what you resist persists. Only by accepting reality can you then create something new.

Acceptance is not giving up. Acceptance is a state of truce with what already exists. Once you stop fighting with your humanity, you can move forward in a new, collaborative effort. Your body is not an enemy. It is the physicality of your mind, thoughts, and beliefs. If you want to be happier, more peaceful, and more fulfilled in this life, you have to bring these ideas into your body. To do this call a truce and begin to work *with* your body instead of forcing decisions upon it. Talk to your body, share your desires with it, and learn to work together to achieve your outcome.

Your body did not create a state of extra poundage to make your life miserable. On the contrary—your body agreed with your beliefs and actions as you used food to meet your needs for comfort, safety, and love. If you have new ideas now about how you want to live life, and since your body is reflective of what you think and believe and how you act, then it makes sense that your body will agree with you and engage in partnership to move toward your new desired outcome. However, you cannot just make demands of your body as if it were an object. That only creates resistance. Make the effort to get on the same team, moving in the same direction. Be clear that your goal is really about a new physical feeling or experience you are really wanting, not just the better body.

Before you can repair the relationship with your body, assess where your relationship currently stands. Go to the mirror, look at your body, and become aware of your initial thoughts. Write down those thoughts and bring them out into the world where you can look at them with new perspective. See exactly what it is you say to yourself consciously and unconsciously.

What I say to myself is:

_____

_____

_____

_____

_____

_____

_____

If you look closely, you will notice that your desire to eat differently and to lose weight is reflective of your desire to generate a new relationship to life. After all, the relationship you have with your body mirrors the relationship you have with life. What you believe about your body, how harmoniously you live with your body, is similar to the relationship you have with greater life. Do you trust your body, and do you trust life? Are you safe in this world and does your body reflect those beliefs? Can you feel good inside of your body and inside of life? To develop a richer, more abundant relationship, review the characteristics that make you a worthwhile, beautiful, living human being. Instead of seeing yourself as a bunch of mismatched parts, see yourself as a whole person. List what is amazing or beneficial about having a body. Right now there might only be a few things that you can think of, but that is a start. How do your physical senses contribute to the beauty of your life? Take one minute and speak appreciative thoughts to yourself and your body. Take risks and feel good, even just a tiny bit good, in your body right now, just as it is.

What is good about being human, about having a body?

_____

_____

_____

_____

_____

_____

_____

Goals Teach You How to Feel Better Today

Are you enjoying life right now? Are you happy in your relationship with your self? You can lead an extraordinary life. Turning your challenges around is possible. But there is a catch: It will not happen on its own. If you want to enjoy greater inner peace, contentment, and fulfillment with your life, you are going to have to shift your focus from everything that is going wrong and place attention on what you could do right now to feel even a small bit more confident or hopeful. Setting goals helps you do this by helping you define your dreams, gain a sense of purpose and direction, and then choose an action step that makes you feel a little better right now.

It is wonderful to anticipate the arrival of your goals; however, goals teach you not to postpone self-love and happiness until the end of your journey. It is necessary to experience them now. Instead of focusing on what you want to banish from your life, goals teach you to focus on actions and choices that add to your life. Goals also show you that to allow good things into your life, you must find yourself deserving. You can become your own best friend and unwavering supporter of yourself. Goals help you discover how to make daily decisions that allow you to reprogram yourself to believe that you are deserving of having what you want. You are deserving of feeling good in your body, worthy of focusing on success, and worthy of your own love and appreciation. Although it may require effort and perseverance, you can determine how you want to feel and then take daily actions that promote those feelings.

Achieving what you want requires forming a relationship with your aspiration. When you do not, you try to simply bully yourself into eating differently and terrorize your body into cooperating. Assuming an authoritarian relationship, you mistakenly believe the only way to have what you want is to have power over things. Harsh, disciplinarian relationships may make you feel temporarily in control and powerful, but they do not lead to lasting empowerment or joy.

Luckily, there is another way! Consider creating a great relationship with intimacy, heart, and soul between you and your goal, you and your body, you and your life. In truth, the idea of what you want is alive in your imagination; however, it is not yet a reality in your body or your physical life. This means that you have to go through a process to foster it. If you attempt to force something to join with you, do not expect balance, harmony, and peace. Instead, expect resistance and conflict. Alternately, if you create an intimate relationship with your desire, if you nurture and love your idea, you will find symbiosis. A partnership is born in which you love your idea and your idea loves you; you love your body and your body accepts your plan; you love your life and your life becomes a reflection of your dreams.

Have you ever really stopped and thought about it—what do you need in order to feel good? The answer lies in combining spirit with body in a manner that allows the creation of desired outcomes. Ending overeating, having a newly shaped body, or any other single accomplishment does not create happiness. Happiness is a function of how much spirit and love you put into the process of creating a new eating style, a newly shaped body, or an achievement. Active engagement in the process of making your dreams become real provides the feeling of being more alive and joyful. In fact, it does not matter if your goal includes getting the dishes washed, creating a life without overeating, or closing multi-million dollar deals. What matters most is how much spirit you bring to the process and how alive and passionate you were during the creation of something new. Yes, the end is important, for in achieving a goal, you have found yourself worthy of receiving it. Yet, it is the discoveries along the way that are the point of the journey. If you bring spirit into the process, then your life becomes joyful.

One important reason goal-setters achieve such outstanding results is that they have learned how to focus their time, energy, and resources on a single objective, even if it is just for a few minutes at a time. This passionate concentration allows success to emerge. As you work through this book, you will start to see possibilities you had never recognized. You will find yourself in the flow of things, experiencing the synchronicity of meaningful coincidences. As you become aware of these coincidences, you will find yourself looking forward to having more good things happen for you in the future. You will see yourself living your desired outcome and feeling good. These collective experiences activate your impending sense of success. All this generates more positive life-energy to fuel momentum for the next step. Aligning with self-chosen outcomes activates creativity, synchronicity, positive expectation, and a host of other powerful forces available to you.

Benefits of Goal Setting

1. Decide your destiny!

2. Erase feelings of helplessness.

3. Make peace with yourself.

4. Feel better today.

Chapter Two

Make Sure Your Benefits Outweigh Your Costs

——Food and Your Power of Choice——

I don't want to be controlled by food. I just want to feel good. I know there is more to life than this. Although filled with anguish, these are beautiful words. If you have ever spoken similar sentiments, take heart. The fact that you want a better life is an indication of readiness to take your next step. These words offer the promise of unforeseen possibilities. You are aware of your unhappiness, and noticing your negatives is a positive first step. You have become conscious of how bad it feels to feel bad. It takes noticing that you are tired of living a certain way before you can move on to a new phase of life.

One fact must be established before we continue: there is nothing "wrong" with you—your biology, your mind, or your spirit. You are not lazy, damaged, or flawed. Emotional, compulsive, or binge eating behaviors are not a sign of illness. You are not the helpless victim of an invading eating disease. Despite how you may sometimes feel, you are not mentally challenged. Actually, your life journey is evolving perfectly!

At some point in your life you began using food to cope with a painful living situation, a difficult experience, an unresolved internal conflict, or emotional suppression. In response to ongoing frustration, stress, boredom, disappointment, or feeling that your life was out of control you began using food in an often unconscious decision to feel better. Food provided a readily accessible answer to an otherwise unsolvable problem or situation.

Food works in a variety of ways to temporarily block painful feelings and to soothe anxiety. Eating calms, offers distraction, and produces emotional numbness. Eating to the point of physical pain distracts attention away from emotional pain. It can alleviate boredom. It can shift your attention away from feeling tense, frustrated, angry, or depressed—even in times when you cannot name what you are feeling. Eating can induce a drug-like effect that alters the perception of pain. Food can provide an intoxicating sugar rush, the comfortable numbness of an overly full belly, or the calm that comes when carbohydrates trigger the release of the mood-soothing brain chemical serotonin.

It is not a crime to want to feel better, and you are not a bad person for turning to food to ease emotional discomfort. If you could separate judgment, shame, and failure from the eating behavior, it would become apparent that the impetus to the behavior is a deep-seated desire to feel different. Eating has become a conditioned reflex to achieve feelings of pleasure, love, and empowerment. Those are all good things; they are what we all want. You deserve to feel good. Consequently, while certain outcomes may be unwanted, it is important to realize the often unconscious and underlying intent was love, self-preservation, and feeling good.

You are not alone, and many people turn to food to alleviate an uncomfortable emotional state at one time or another. Using food to feel better is not sinful or shameful. You are not a defective person, and there is nothing wrong with you. Turning to food for comfort is a natural attempt to feel better. It is acceptable, normal even, to eat when your body feels different from usual. For many people, eating has never been simply about satisfying physical hunger. It is estimated that over half of all adults turn to food to manage a negative mood. Furthermore, from our earliest experiences, food has played an important role in nourishing the soul as well as the body. We share casseroles during times of loss, eat cake to celebrate life, nervously munch on appetizers at cocktail parties, or absentmindedly snack while working on a tight deadline.

Your decision to turn to food was a self-loving choice at the time. Even though you believed yourself unable to find an acceptable outcome to some difficult area of your life, you still found some way of making yourself feel better. Not knowing how to allow your emotions positive expression, unable to assert yourself, unsure of how to soothe and love your self during an uncomfortable experience, you grasped at an external solution. It is a positive action to pursue a means to feeling better. Seeking a tool, even food, to find comfort is understandable. There is no need for life-long analysis of why this happened or who is to blame. The important concept to note is that your food and weight issues are intermixed with other problem areas in your life. Using food was a solution you found to help you survive.

Becoming highly discontent over your eating behaviors is a good sign. It means that you are ready to face your life in a new way. While food and weight may have always been your primary focus, they are secondary consequences of an internal struggle. Using food to provide escape or relief helped you survive life, but now you are ready to move beyond surviving.

Food can provide a short reprieve, a time-out when needed. It may provide momentary sweetness, fullness, or suppression of uncomfortable emotions. However, external pleasures are a waxy substitute for authentic love. It sort of looks and feels like the real thing, but it is not, and we know it. No matter how much food we manage to eat, the pleasure is short-lived. Soon our "fix" runs out, and it is time for another dose of medicine. The pleasure ends, and the hollow absence of self-love and lack of empowerment are more noticeable than ever. Guilt, shame, and unwanted weight gain are the most noticeable long-term results. Stagnated personal growth is another.

Eating to feel better became an action, a well-worn habituated action, to provide momentary relief. While avoidance of unpleasant emotional experiences can be useful in certain situations, it is not useful when the distraction becomes an automatic, long-term coping mechanism. Over time, you become dependent on using food to find gratification, to manage your feelings, or to relieve distress. Continually suppressing emotions by eating creates secondary problems. Avoidance strategies cannot replace the necessity of learning to support yourself—physically, mentally, and spiritually—when experiencing life distresses or emotional upsets.

Your spirit is ready to expand beyond the limitations of your former life. Your life is a continuous process of waking up new potentials, and remembering—at least on the inside—that you have a very important life to enjoy. Imagine finally feeling at home in your own body, filled with delicious passion and joy! Imagine feeling self-love, trust, and confidence and, from that foundation, creating a new life in which you are aligned with energy and purpose!

However, you cannot just end your eating behaviors. To move forward, you must undergo a major shift in how you see the world and your place in it. You must be willing to see that food cannot provide compassion, offer stability, or encourage empowerment. This habit of eating offers only temporary calm and is an unsuccessful replacement for authentic self-love or joy. In addition, little if any attention is given to the physical, sensory pleasure of food while ingesting it, so how could food provide even a remotely adequate substitute for happiness? As the chemical, numbing, or repressing effects of consumption evaporate, the instinctive need for love and empowerment from the *inside* remains unbearably strong.

Food may now be your main source of comfort, your primary nonviolent way of expressing anger or rage, or the best way you know how to deal with depression. Even so, your main issue is not food but learning to live life in a brand-new way. Your objective is not to count calories but to pay attention to the tugging of your spirit. If you convince yourself that nothing is wrong except this infuriating obsession with food you will miss an opportunity to align with important inner values. If you continue to believe that if only you could just conquer your dysfunctional relationship with food and lose weight you would attain somehow a life that is joyous and wonderful, then you miss an opportunity to resolve important inner conflicts.

The personal growth occurring within is a pressing desire to move away from relying on external sources to conjure positive feelings and instead move toward the discovery and expansion of internal love. Either choice—external gratification or internal love—provides an avenue to feeling good. You are not a bad person because you eat in an attempt to feel good. However, your eating habits fail in their long-term ability to provide the inner peace you so desire. When you cannot *feel* the sweetness or fullness of your life on the inside, no amount of food or external substitute can fill the hole of what is missing.

Ending your eating behaviors is a difficult process but is also an exciting occasion to gain new vision, greater confidence, and the ability to be in control of your destiny. Rest assured, even with the ingrained habit of your eating actions, you can move forward into the life of your dreams. Keep in mind that no matter how difficult achieving your goal is, this opportunity of transformation is a gift given to you by you! You are ready to move beyond your old life. You have brought yourself to this place of change. Discover the greatest secret of all humanity . . . that you are the source of love, the center of your experience, and the creator of new experiences.

Redefine Love

Congratulations on waking up each morning and greeting the day with renewed determination! Perhaps you rise and say, "Today is the day—I will make it through the entire day sticking to my diet goals." What a wonderful, optimistic way to begin a fresh day! Ahead of you lies the promise of a clean start. Unfortunately, experience has shown that good intentions alone are not enough to overpower the urge to binge. In a moment of crisis, focus and optimism seem to disappear. This is when positivity needs to be coupled with a sound plan. Willpower alone is not enough to overcome a craving or the desire to use food as a way to escape reality. What provides extra empowerment is a predetermined, personalized plan of action where you know what you are moving toward coupled with a powerfully motivating reason to press forward.

Believe it or not, the part of you that woke up this morning and firmly stated that today was going to be a success remains with you all day. A part of you does want to make it through the day without overeating. Hidden somewhere underneath the overwhelming urge to eat is that aspect of you that was confident as you began the day. It is going to be your primary task to actively seek and strengthen that part of yourself. To accomplish this, you are going to need to couple your confidence with lots of love and self-care. The midst of a crisis is no time to try to learn this skill. Rather, you develop your skills during the times you feel strong and confident so they will be at your disposal when they are needed.

To be successful with your goal, realize that using food for comfort occurred as a result of sacrificing your own needs and desires for that of others. You became an expert at delaying your needs or self-expression and then attempted to make it all okay with food. It is important that you now begin to shift the focus of your goal away from "dieting" toward new ways of loving yourself, taking care of your needs, articulating your desires, and allowing yourself pleasure.

Learning new patterns of activating love involves having an awareness of what self-love is and then practicing certain skills, self-affirming thoughts, and actions that make self-love real. Self-love is not so much a feeling as it is a lessening of self-doubt and self-disapproval. It is a sense of balance and belonging. Respect, responsibility for self, and feeling good become important values. Self-love means that your well-being matters unconditionally and in practical terms. The following are some characteristics of self-loving people:

- Self-loving people tend to treat themselves well.

- They see enjoyment of life as a primary goal most of the time.

- They do not remain in mistreatment by others.

- They are caring towards others, not because they have to be, but as a natural overflow of their own self-love.

- They put themselves first—even those they love are a "close second."

- They find a thought that feels good and practice it.

- They focus on actions that expand their sense of purpose and fulfillment.

How much time and energy do you devote to yourself? Oh sure, you bathe, groom, keep yourself and your environment generally clean and neat. However, that is not what we are talking about here. What we are discussing is what you need to give to yourself on a monthly, daily, and even hourly basis to keep your body, spirit, and intellect well loved. If you do not attend to your needs, you will continue to require relying on food for comfort. The heart of any goal process teaches you the basic principles of self-love and self-caring:

- Who you are is more important than what you are.

- You are valuable. Nothing can change that.

- What you want always matters.

If you are like most of us, you have experienced self-love, at least a little. However, have you found your way to experience the everyday flow of love that fills your body? Are you able to find this love when you need it most? This love comes from the inside. There is no event, person, or external stimulus that can manufacture this feeling. There is no prerequisite that will make you worthy of love, nor is it something to be earned. You do not have to be thin enough, rich enough, good enough, nice enough, or even pretty enough to have this love. Additionally, love and happiness do not suddenly appear at the end of your goal.

Logically, it would seem that you would gladly allow yourself to feel love. Yet, this is often not the case. You have learned to focus on the negative. You may say you want to feel happy but then do anything you can to avoid it. You allow yourself to tolerate pain and discomfort. You cling to worries. You permit your mind to dwell on unhappy thoughts. Amazingly, you have become an expert on postponing love. Maybe you see yourself in some of these examples:

- Waiting until losing weight before dressing comfortably and attractively.

- Not persevering with promises to self.

- Not setting or achieving your goals.

- Thinking the love and joy will come once you have achieved the goal.

- Self-criticizing for each step of your goal not accomplished perfectly.

- Not acknowledging individual effort or success.

- Eating wonderful meals only when in the company of others.

- Cooking for others but not for you.

- Not allowing time for creative expression.

- Tolerating poor treatment from others.

- Tolerating poor treatment from yourself.

- An almost total absence of self-care.

- Isolating yourself because you have decided you are not worthy of being with other people in your current state.

Each of us has the capacity increase our ability to feel love from the inside out. Turning your life into a passion-filled, exciting adventure *is* possible, but only when you align with choices that bring greater happiness into your now reality. You may currently be using food to bring pleasure, but it is a short-lived pleasure that is used to alleviate stress, mask boredom, or dilute uncomfortable emotions. Love unfolds as you value your own needs, as you set a direction in life, and then take self-supportive actions that bring more empowerment, inner peace, or pride. This decision to take self-caring actions that feel good must happen repeatedly.

It seems a common practice to force our bodies into some sort of change or weight loss and then expect to feel good at the end. Feeling good is not something that happens to you. It is not something that magically occurs at the end of any achievement. Instead, feeling good is a matter of allowing enjoyment, satisfaction, and fulfillment. Feeling good involves choosing a direction or pursuit that has meaning to you and then making that journey as filled with pleasure as possible. Pleasure is a tangible, physical body experience. For example, what do you see, hear, feel, smell, taste, and know, right now, in this moment? Are you making choices today that align with personal values and desires, and how do those choices feel in your body?

Without making your experience right or wrong, good or bad, allow yourself to become aware of your senses in the present moment. Rather than dwelling on the past or worrying about the future, simply permit yourself to be aware of the energy of life. If you are not feeling well, stop and look around. There is beauty all around you and within you. Submit yourself to the sensation of being filled by the abundance that is already present in your life and be nourished by it. When you consciously activate your senses and fill them with beautiful sights, smells, and sounds, your feelings of well-being will increase. You will be less likely to think that something is wrong with you or that you cannot have what you want. The more you engage you senses, the more you will realize how much happiness is under your control.

Achieving your goal is a process through which you teach yourself to enlarge your love of self. You learn how to work with your emotions, clarify your values, decide your outcome, and take daily actions that help you move toward your dreams. Meanwhile, you learn to fuel your life with new relaxation strategies. You discover new ways of feeling good in the short-term that do not lead to long-term undesired consequences.

What are some of the ways you hold yourself back from love, self-care, and feeling good?

1. _____
2. _____
3. _____
4. _____
5. _____

What are some ways you can increase your level of love, self-care, and feeling good?

1. _____
2. _____
3. _____
4. _____
5. _____

Develop a New Relationship with Yourself

Setting goals is an amazing tool that can open your heart and unleash new possibilities. During the process, you teach yourself how to listen to your spirit, nourish your body, and teach your mind to focus on a new reality. One of the primary benefits of goal setting is that you learn to be a priority in your own life. Your happiness and success depend on developing a new relationship between yourself and your environment, yourself and your desires, and yourself and your body. Incorporating some or all of the following actions will make achieving your goals easier:

Create a personal sanctuary by setting aside a special place in your home. This safe haven may be an entire room or may be just the corner of a bedroom. By creating a private personalized place, you bring your unique creativity and values into the world. On a very small scale, you establish your authentic presence. However, your small-scale actions have large-scale implications. When you take action to design a space that looks, feels, and smells exactly the way you want it to, you form a new relationship between yourself and life. You find that you can bring harmony into the world and that you do know what you like and what feels good to you. You can claim your territory and know that you belong here. You can bring new creative ideas to expression.

Put real effort into creating the right sacred space for you. Experiment with paint colors or curtain fabrics, go wild and buy a comfortable chair without asking anyone else's opinion or permission. Add your grandmother's quilt, a favorite childhood stuffed animal, meaningful artwork, your baby photographs, your favorite rocks, inspirational books and quotes, and life-awakening music. It is important to have a separate space, a peaceful place, with room to relax and create.

Keep an ongoing journal. If you struggle with food, confidence, and self-image, then you have become a master at "safely" tucking away your feelings. However, just because you suppress your emotions does not mean that they disappear. In fact, they usually remain trapped. I once read that we are only as sick as our secrets. Holding back thoughts and emotions causes them to become secrets. Instead of learning to see the wisdom within them, you become a silent negative thinker, wary of the emotions your body is holding onto. Those thoughts and emotions do not go away, instead they linger, fester, and gnaw at you all day long.

Writing is a powerful form of personal exploration. This form of self-expression brings thoughts, ideas, and feelings out into the world. When you can see what you are thinking, you can work with things in a whole new way. You gain power to choose how to respond, rather than letting your internal scripting decide for you. You can go beyond a superficial response to life and work out values and convictions. In this way, you gain control and discover who you are at your core.

Simply write down whatever comes to mind, include your favorite quotes, or track your dreams. Forget about neatness or spelling. Instead, give yourself space to express yourself with loud, honest boldness. In your journal you do not have to be mature and responsible. Make a big deal about your petty thoughts, express your anger in thunderous black crayons, release your frustration by scribbling frantically all over the pretty paper, note your joy and successes with pictures and daring exclamation marks. Writing can be a powerful step into self-expression and seeing that you always have the power of choice.

If you find yourself resistant to writing in a journal or unable to write anything on those blank pages, take heart. Notice that you have guarded certain areas of your self-expression. Perhaps this served a useful purpose during your upbringing. However, now that you are an adult this choice may no longer serve your need for authenticity or unique expression. You have important things to say and articulate. Writing is one tool that can open that doorway once again.

Initiate a morning ritual of sitting quietly. Sit quietly, even if only for one minute, before walking out the door. This one minute may be the most important minute of your day. Sit down and simply breathe. This can help slow your mind, lift you out of old habits of stress and rushing, and create balance. Take a minute to touch base with you. You can ask, what is going on with me? What am I feeling? What do I want to do today? Sitting down for even just one minute before meeting the demands of your busy life can allow you to pay attention to what is meaningful to you. You can look forward to what the new day has to offer before rushing off into it helter-skelter. I have changed the way I view mornings by remembering the following inspiring words by J.B. Priestly, "I have always been delighted at the prospect of a new day, a fresh try, one more start, with perhaps a bit of magic waiting somewhere behind the morning."

Create a comfort drawer. First, obtain an empty box, drawer, or large file folder. In it put cards from loved ones, memos about a job well done, or favorite photos. Place in your comfort drawer whatever makes you feel good about who you are or reminds you of the people you are connected with and the wonderful times you have had in life. During your goal-achieving process, whenever you are feeling down or uncertain, open your comfort drawer and look at several of your items. It is easy to lose track of yourself when facing a challenge. Taking the time to reflect on your life helps bring you back to the bigger picture. Things are not always difficult, and this too shall pass. Looking back at your achievements and memorable connections can help you gain confidence in a brighter future.

Actively seek to increase your daily experiences of joy. If you have taken a few detours in life, perhaps forgotten your true purpose, or are feeling lost and empty, do not worry so much. Everything is alright, and all your experiences are immensely valuable, even if you cannot see it in this exact moment. You will. You are a capable, empowered, self-adjusting, self-balancing human being. You are already in the process of setting yourself back on an appropriate course. Take a breath and realize that everything is alright, even though everything in your life is not exactly as you would wish. Begin to focus more intently on generating emotions that feel good. Putting your entire attention on the final goal, delaying satisfaction until reaching a final point of success, and moti- vating your self with force takes all the life out of your journey. It is hard to know you are winning, and even harder to keep going in the absence of acknowledgment of success and rewards. When you do not think you are making progress, it is easy to quit and walk away. Learning to feel good along the way generates the power of accomplishment.

Most of us do not pay attention to the smaller, day-to-day occurrences that make us happy. We tend to focus on the negative and, all too easily, share all the things that go wrong. We have selective memory and remember our struggles more vividly than life situations that flowed smoothly. It is easy to take for granted the goodness and joy that is already available in our lives, while getting lost in a torrent of emotional wounds, anxiety about problems, and other negative thoughts.

To overcome this tendency, become a person who goes out into the world deliberately searching for positive experiences. Actively seek opportunities to improve your lot on a daily basis. Smell the delicious aroma of your food, taste the robustness of your coffee, or smile at the grocery cashier. Receive compliments and provide heartfelt acts of kindness. It does not matter how big or small the gesture. Just take control and acknowledge life experiences that feel good to you. Happiness involves developing a sensory relationship with life itself and knowing that you are connected to the physicality of earth. To reinforce this new pattern of opening your body to receive joy, consider adding a few of these choices into your daily diet:

- Eat delicious food and activate every sense while eating.

- Sing from your heart and dance from your soul.

- Do kind things for yourself.

- Engage in activities that make you *feel* great to be alive.

- Give yourself positive feedback.

- Take action on the goals that are important to you.

- Learn to relieve stress.

Decide that you deserve to feel good in life. Take a few moments to sit still, breathe deeply, and relax even just a little. Notice what is right with the world, engage your senses, and open up to the goodness already present. It may be cliché, but when you stop to smell the roses, the world really is a brighter, happier place to live in. As you read the rest of this book, design goals and daily actions steps that you believe will contribute to your enjoyment of your body and life. Activate the power of imagination. What would an enjoyable life look like? What thoughts and dreams warm your heart and invite your spirit? What could you do today that would make you feel gladder to be alive? When you deliberately focus your attention on the positive, purposely seeking the aspects of life that you crave, you will find that they are already here. Reflecting on what is right with your world and with yourself results in greater enthusiasm, determination, joy, serenity, and energy.

Speak positive thoughts to yourself. Forget spending time trying to erase negative thought patterns. Instead, spend your time learning to support yourself during the good times and the bad. A habit that may sound silly at first but one that will be invaluable throughout your lifetime, is walking up to a mirror and talking to your self and your body. Instead of always being in combat with your behaviors and your body, develop a new relationship. Let yourself know that you are choosing to be alive in a new way. Let yourself know that what you want is important. Even when you fail, you are worthy of your own support and love.

Gently speak to your body and remind it of your overall goal. Remember with kindness that you are asking it to change and do things differently. Provide reassurance to your body that it is doing a good job. Do the same for your mind. They both depend on your leadership, your commitment to your outcome, and your love for encouragement and motivation. Do not be afraid to share your love and compassion with all parts of yourself. Even though you are an adult now, you still need care and nurturing. You are responsible for seeing that your needs are met. You are responsible for providing encouragement and support. Taking the time to take care of your self with positive encouragement will begin the process of filling the void and emptiness within.

Acknowledge the whole truth about yourself at least weekly. If you cannot stop obsessing about what is wrong with you, then that is okay. However, make a consistent effort to balance the equation by also acknowledging what is right with you. Take time to recognize the characteristics that make you unique. Use a mirror to look at yourself as a whole person and explicitly state beautiful truths about yourself. Learn to connect with yourself on a regular basis.

Instead of constantly worrying and stressing, set aside time each day to envision a new life. Take a moment to relish the physical sensations of the anticipation of your exciting dream. The idea of losing weight is not very exciting; however, visualizing a new life of your choosing is exciting. Imagine yourself in your ideal life. Touch your body lovingly, breathe in the love for yourself, and feel the safety and comfort of living inside your body. Develop a loving relationship with your dream, and learn to support yourself in many different ways as you move forward toward your goal.

Three Principles of Love

• **Who you are is more important than what you are.**

• **You are valuable. Nothing can change that.**

• **What you want always matters.**

Chapter Three

Why Most Goals Do Not Work

—Identify Your Underlying Motivations—

How many times have you set a goal but ended up losing sight of what you wanted and, in the end, never accomplished it? How many times have you quit your diet, blaming yourself for not saying enough affirmations or not trying hard enough? Perhaps you even think something is wrong with you or that you do not deserve to have what you want. Alternately, there have been many times in your life when you set a goal and you actually did an excellent job of succeeding. You reached your goal, and yet something about it did not feel complete. Perhaps the victory felt hollow or even disappointing. You did an outstanding job of getting what you thought you wanted, which was weight loss, but when you accomplished the goal, it was not what you anticipated. It was not the *essence* of what you wanted.

The one main reason that goals fail is that we do not understand that change, for its own sake, is not the real reason we set the goal. You are not *just* trying to be thin or end overeating. There is a reason beneath the reason. In other words, there is a compelling reason that is so important to you that you would spend the rest of your life working to obtain it. Often, this fundamental core reason lies concealed and hidden beneath your desire to eat differently or lose weight.

Have you ever heard the sales and marketing expression, "Sell the sizzle, not the steak?" This aphorism tells us something important about human nature. It tells us that it is not the thing you are selling that inspires a customer's desire for it but rather the anticipated feelings that they will experience as a result of having it. In other words, emotional and sensory experience motivates us. When you set a goal that involves food and weight, sure you want "thinness" or "ending overeating"—that is the "steak"! However, the "sizzle" is the rich feeling and enjoyable emotional experience obtained through your journey. The "sizzle" does not suddenly appear at the end of your journey, it is the feeling or experience of what you want to enlarge with every step of your journey.

Sticking with the steak theme, imagine anticipating the finest aged, succulent U.S. Prime steak, broiled to perfection, seasoned expertly, tender and juicy, and served just the way you like. (If you are vegetarian, substitute your favorite food into this example.) Your steak is delivered to your table, artfully prepared to enhance its flavors and provide a mouth-watering experience. The surrounding ambiance offers the ideal balance of romance and intimacy that promises you a great time and great memories. Candlelight, background music, and the wonderful aroma of your steak fill your senses. Of course, you want the steak! However, imagine an identical steak only this time served without the full physical-sensory experiences. There is no atmosphere, no enjoyable mood. There is no white tablecloth and no candles or roses in front of you. The room is quiet and so dark you cannot even see your steak. You have a sinus infection resulting in nasal congestion, a limited capacity to smell, and decreased taste. You eat the steak and it fills your stomach. Same steak, only this time it is not a satisfying experience.

The same is true with your weight loss goals. If you manage to reach the end of your goal without giving yourself the physical and emotional experiences you were searching for, your goal will end up being an unfulfilling, unsatisfying experience. You want the "sizzle"—the benefits of your change—while you are taking your journey. You want to have the daily experiences of your life being a little better, a little more hopeful, a little more empowered. Yes, of course your basic desire is valid and real. You want to end overeating, or you want to have a different size body. However, you also want and need to experience an ever-increasing ability to feel differently and live differently.

For example, imagine a friend confessing the following to you:

"I am a victim of an abusive relationship. I eat to relieve anxiety; I eat when I am upset. I have gained weight, and now I do not want to go out anymore. I am depressed and use food to comfort myself. I know I am punishing myself, and I want to quit this type of eating. I do not love myself. I do not want anyone to see me. I do not even look in a mirror. If only I could lose weight, my life would be better."

This is a perfect example illustrating that the issue *is* about ending the overeating, but also so much more than that. For your friend to succeed and shed the shell that keeps her isolated from people, she would also need to develop new ways to feel safe in the world and relaxed in her body. Underneath her goal is her desire to build new life skills and perhaps gain new assertiveness qualities. If she sets a goal to simply lose weight, her journey will be complicated by the fact that losing weight will require her to be able to manage increased attention. She will also have to comfort herself without food as her coping mechanism. Rather than attacking her "weight problem," if she realizes that what she wants is to feel differently about herself and take care of herself in new ways, then she will make choices that bring her closer to the underlying benefits she had wanted all along.

One part of her goal *is* about ending undesired eating behaviors, but what is important underneath is her yearning to feel more peace and safety in her body and life than she is currently experiencing. If she is only aware of her desire to lose weight and stop overeating, there is a chance she may succeed, at least temporarily. Yet, a permanent resolution will occur only if she is consciously aware that pursuing her goal is her attempt to gain a sense of empowerment, establish greater authority over her life experiences, expand her capacity to love herself, feel worthy, and be in charge of her body and her happiness.

That is just one example. Not everyone who is trying to change overeating is dealing with abuse issues. Nevertheless, every goal, no matter who is setting it or its specifics, is a desire to grow and expand our capacity to enjoy life. It does not matter how big or how small the goal is. If you set a goal, you have some core and compelling reason that is vital to adding meaning and depth to your life journey. If you are not consciously aware of that sizzle—the promise you have offered yourself—you are either going to fail to achieve permanent success or your achievement will feel disappointing.

Beneath every goal is an attempt to enjoy one of more of the following experiences:

- Moving beyond current assumptions and perceptions about the world, others, and self

- Moving beyond conditioned responses

- Increasing focus on personal values

- Releasing negative internal dialogue or a self-critical attitude

- Building a sound, harmonious relationship with self, others, and the environment

- Being able to think differently and bigger

- Becoming more spontaneous, adventurous, or passionate

- Solving problems in a new way

- Gaining self-initiative

- Making choices that do not leave you feeling helpless and fragmented

Over the years, we have all collected a series of assumptions, beliefs, and expectations about how life works, who we are, who we should be, and how to make decisions. Over time, we outgrow many of these truths and formulas. Setting goals is one way in which we go through a process to uncover what we believe and replace those concepts with updated, more self-supporting beliefs.

One day you will get to the end of your life; and, on that day, you will want to be able to say, "Wow! What a journey! I did exactly what I came here to do. I grew in ways that were important to me." This type of long-term success requires that you tap into not just the most obvious reasons for your ambition but the single compelling reason behind it. By defining your purpose explicitly, you can become incredibly clear on why you are willing to put so much effort and determination into your goal. With this compelling reason, you will know that no matter what happens, no matter how long it takes or what effort you must exert, you will not give up until you have the outcome that was so important to you all along.

It's All About Feeling Better

People who have an emotional attachment to food eat because they do not know another way to cope with what they are *feeling or experiencing*. Some people eat to find comfort, to repress sexuality, or to punish themselves for perceived failures. Other reasons people turn to food include the following:

- Stress, tension, anxiety, fear, or frustration

- Boredom; not being focused on a purpose in life

- Depression or feeling blue

- Fatigue or having low energy levels

- Unmet needs for fun, play, or excitement

- Excessive busyness; a life out of balance

- A desire for love, romance, or intimacy

- Anger, resentment, or bitterness

- Emptiness or loneliness

- Shame: self-blame, low self-esteem, self-loathing, or unworthiness

What are some of the reasons that you eat the way you do?

1. _____

2. _____

3. _____

4. _____

5. _____

Well before the eating became habitual, you began by simply feeling emotional discomfort and choosing a behavior, in this case eating, to cope with the feeling. The behavior provided a temporary reprieve from pain, and you automatically returned to the behavior again and again. Soon, the behavior became an automatic response to any difficulty. As a result, you cannot plan to only change the eating behavior. You must acquire a greater capacity to handle life so that you will not turn to eating as a solution. In constructing a plan of action to overcome the behavior, you must take into account the less obvious personality traits that you want to cultivate. If you simply fix the problem of eating, you have missed your primary intention—to acquire the ability to adapt to stressful situations, resolve existing anxieties, and create new ways of looking at the world.

You set goals to develop a new perspective from which to understand and work with your emotions, spirit, and body. In addition, your goal is designed to build greater core inner strength. Each step along the way will provide the exact appropriate obstacles, challenges, and failures for you to face what you currently believe about yourself, the world, and the way it works. That is why the process is difficult, and that is why shortcuts do not work. Pursuing self-improvement is how you unearth deep-seated notions about what is or is not possible, what you are or are not capable of doing.

Believe it or not, the purpose of aspiring to a goal is to challenge entrenched and limiting assumptions. On some level, you have grown tired of your constrained outlook on the world and your possibilities within it. Yet, limiting beliefs do not evaporate simply because they no longer work for you. On the contrary, they live deep inside of you, governing your emotions, thoughts, and actions. By purposefully setting out to make a change, such as ending overeating, you are actually excavating these constraints and exposing them each time you meet a challenge or setback.

Self-limiting beliefs are the set of internal, perceived truths that place restrictions on your abilities. These assumptions automatically shift your focus in a certain direction that, in turn, determines your decisions, actions, or inactions. Limiting beliefs blind you to other possibilities. For instance, they determine your automatic internal dialogue when you come face-to-face with difficulty, failure, or emotional pain. It is your embedded beliefs and your subsequent way of thinking that persuades you that you are powerless to create change in your life.

There are as many versions of limiting beliefs as there are people in the world. However, you may be familiar with a few common versions of limiting beliefs:

- I feel completely helpless.

- I will not make it; there is no way out.

- Things are beyond my control.

- There is no point in trying because nothing ever works.

- I will not get any better.

- I hate life; I hate myself because I cannot have what I want.

- I am not safe; I cannot feel good.

- Whatever I do, it does not help.

- It is not fair that I have to face this challenge.

- It is just too much.

- No one supports me in this goal.

- I cannot take it any more.

- Nobody is helping me; nobody gives a damn about me.

- I want to curl up and never move again.

- I have lost all hope.

- Why me? Why is this happening to me?

What do you tell yourself when you face a difficult emotion, situation, or challenge? What do you say to yourself right before you reach for food? What do you say to yourself when you try to stop yourself from taking that first bite? What does your inner voice say when you experience a setback or failure? To answer these questions, allow yourself to have the experience. Only, instead of trying to change it, allow yourself to be self-aware and curious. Ask yourself, "What is it I believe about myself, the world, or other people during this experience? What am I saying inside?"

You may want to bookmark these examples of limiting beliefs and refer to them as you pursue your goal and encounter inner resistance. As painful as these beliefs are, the purpose of your journey is to face what you believe about life and about yourself and then move beyond those limits by making new decisions. List any limiting beliefs that you may already recognize within yourself:

1. _____

2. _____

3. _____

4. _____

5. _____

People set goals because something in their lives leaves them feeling powerless. Right now, this sense of lost control and your eating behaviors are connected. No matter what you have tried or how hard you have tried, your eating patterns or weight continues to feel overwhelming. You set goals because you want to show yourself that what you believe is not true. You no longer want to believe you are powerless or unable to change how you feel or act. Although your goal is difficult, from a larger perspective, that is the beauty of goals: you are always on a path of perpetual exploration and expansion, always seeking new adventures into what might be possible.

If you are reading this book, your current adventure is to see if you can shed the self-limiting beliefs connected with your food, eating, or weight challenge. As you begin, it helps to acknowledge that the point of your journey is to discover the places in which you believe yourself to be powerless. You are asking yourself to face difficult, inner assumptions and beliefs. As you face them, only you can decide whether to continue agreeing with your self-limiting beliefs or whether to support your dreams by taking positive action even during the difficult times. By moving forward even when things seem most hopeless, you replace limiting beliefs with more self-supporting and empowering ideas.

Here is how it works: You set a goal and think the goal is about trying to stop eating in a certain manner or is about trying to lose weight. While that is true, the compelling reason is in shedding some old belief that once served your needs but now only holds you back. Therefore, you set the goal and soon encounter a challenge or experience failure. Poof! Your limiting belief instantly rises to the surface. Your inner voice tells you that you cannot handle this challenge. You feel despair, helplessness, and isolation. The anguish you feel is your limiting belief asserting itself. Unbelievably, this is exactly what you want to happen. You are now allowing yourself to face your belief and its associated thoughts and emotions.

As your despair overtakes you, you will crave the old coping mechanism or eating behavior to feel better. This is the decisive moment to change your typical behavior—or not to change. If you give in and resort to some type of overeating, you miss the opportunity to weaken a limiting belief. If you become overwhelmed, stressed, collapse, give up, or sink into depression, you have confirmed your fears. You validate that you are a victim to your situation. You drop the objective you desire, and your old patterns reassert themselves as useful and comforting. You resume your life as it was before your goal and all is well—until you meet your next challenge or pick up the goal once again.

The above scenario is typical. You gather the courage to face your fear, and then get scared as it comes out of hiding. This *is* a frightening experience. If you fail, do not beat yourself up. Yes, you have failed in your most recent attempt to face your belief, but this is how the process is supposed to work! Even if you have not been able to achieve a goal thus far, you still have not completely given up. When you are ready and you have gathered renewed strength and determination, you will begin again.

One day, you will set the goal and almost certainly experience a challenge or even failure. That same old way of thinking will rise to the surface as it always does. Your inner voice will tell you that you cannot handle this challenge, and you feel the familiar helpless, hopeless, or despairing feelings. You will experience fear, emotional pain, and anxiety. You will want to rely on the old way and run away from this challenge . . . only this time, you will take a breath, remember why this moment is so important, and choose differently.

As you take an action that moves you through the fear or resistance, you realize you are not helpless, life is not hopeless, and you are worthy of having what you want. The moment you move past a limiting belief, you realize that just like the cowardly lion in *The Wizard of Oz*, you had courage all along. Facing what you fear is the very reason you set your goal and the single most important step in achieving it. That is one aspect of what is so beautiful about humanity: we have the perseverance to do whatever it takes, for as long as it takes, to free ourselves from our own prisons.

When You Are Willing to Do Whatever It Takes, You Know Your Core Motivation

The purpose of core motivation is to help you shed a self-limiting belief and position a new, more self-supporting principle in its place. For example, if you are aware that you have a fear of failure, you realize that your compelling reason for setting the goal is: 1) to experience failure so that you will learn to define it in a new way, perhaps as a necessary source of feedback, and then, because of this new definition, 2) to allow yourself to succeed.

To discover your core motivation, you first accept that what is true today does not have to be true forever. Realize that as you set forth toward your goal, you will most certainly reach a point where moving forward seems impossible. You will find yourself stuck, overwhelmed, and possibly even feeling hopeless. Incredible as it seems, you have been waiting for this moment. Setting a goal brings you into the exact challenge that will bring your most painful self-limiting beliefs into the forefront. You will face a wall, feel trapped, and not know what to do next. If you face this moment without collapsing into hopelessness, self-pity, or depression, you empower yourself to make a different choice. You can stand there, facing your wall, and decide not to give up or give in. You may not know what to do next, but you can stand there and love yourself for having reached this point. In addition, you can breathe and trust that soon you will find your next creative, possible solution to this problem. In this approach, you are able to gain confidence, hone your optimism, and form a new attitude. As you can see, an awareness of your compelling reason for wanting to reach your goal is essential. It provides the moment for you to decide to stop working on your issue and get earnest about having what you want.

No matter how much you have learned or how much you understand about why you eat the way you do, your behavior exists because you *live* a belief about yourself or the world. For example, your belief may be, "There is no point in trying to change because nothing ever works." As you move forward on your goal and face an inevitable challenge, your belief will rise to the surface. Hearing the "truth" of what you believe, you will be tempted to quit. After all, this is what you believe, and what would be the point of continuing?

If you give up on your goal, your belief, and the associated feelings, stressful thoughts and behaviors go back into hiding. You will feel temporarily better as your conflict subsides. That is not the same as letting the belief go for good. The only way to release a belief is to call it forth and move beyond it. It will not be easy those first few times you say "no" to the behavior of compulsive eating and "yes" to your new idea that your efforts do indeed make a difference. If you really want to free yourself from being a prisoner to your behavior, you have to challenge what you believe. I wish I could say differently, but truly the only way out is through.

Once you have said "no more!" to your behavior and meant it, you will face tremendous temptation to turn to the old patterns of behavior. By refusing to allow yourself to cope in these tried-and-true ways, you will be uncomfortable. You will not think you have the fortitude to stand strong. However, this time you will not give in to the eating behavior. You might pace. You will likely feel anger with both yourself and the behavior. You will want to escape having to stand by your decision. You will feel like a powerless victim. You might even rather die than go through that moment, but you will not die, and you will not give up.

This time you will stop trying to rely on *willpower* and instead engage your **will**. Will is simply saying, "May what I desire be done." What I have promised myself I will do, I will complete. Will states, "I am scared, and I do not want to face my emotions and fears, but this time, I am going to stand here and say 'yes' to my decision. No matter how loud my worn-out belief is, and no matter how difficult this process is, I have decided to face myself and make a new decision." That day will be the turning point of your life.

On that day, you will face your limiting belief. It will become apparent how powerful your belief is, and how strongly your associated thought patterns govern your emotions and actions. Yet, bravely you will make the decision to take a new direction. You will say to yourself, "I can have what I want. I am not a victim of life, of my body, or even of food." As you choose differently, you accept the inner strength you had been avoiding or pretending that you did not have. You acknowledge that you made a decision and that now you accept the power to follow through with that decision. You are not weak, you are not helpless, and you are not a victim. These illusions will fall away.

If you do not take the time to uncover your compelling reason for change, you will find it difficult, if not impossible, to face this moment and choose a new direction. Instead, you will give in to the behavior but continue to "work" on your goal. The underlying reason for the issue you are trying to change will remain. Realize however, that "working" on your issue does not prove anything to anyone. It does not make you a better person. It does not buy sympathy or points for good behavior. It does not expand your joy or lead to a more empowered life. As long as you are "working" on your goal, you remain a perpetual student in your own life—always busy battling or pretending to reach your outcome but never allowing yourself to have what you want.

By simply attacking the behavior, devoid of the core cause, your achievements will be temporary. You will not achieve full development as a person who actively, passionately, and determinedly engages in the deliberate formation of a better life. That is the heart of goal setting—overcoming the resistance to releasing the known and allowing yourself to venture into untested waters. You trade your old beliefs for ones that support, motivate, encourage, and inspire a positive future. You want not only success but the expansion of confidence, self-love, empowerment, and joy.

Why Do You Want What You Want?

The river you want to cross is not too deep, too cold, or too wide. You really can get to the other side. To get there though, you have to *want* to get to the other side. You have to actually step into the river, and no matter how deep, swift, or cold it is, you must doggedly walk or swim until you cross over. It does not matter that other people are not getting in the river with you or making it easier for you. You need only concern yourself with your reason for taking the risk to cross. Without conscious awareness of this compelling reason, you do not have much chance of success. In fact, you may not ever bother to try.

The difficulty in dealing with eating-coping behaviors is that you cannot just decide to give up food. You need to know—in advance—*why* you are giving up food. What are you going to gain during the process that makes giving up food an important decision? The payoff cannot be some illusion that once you have what you want the world will validate you and happiness will ensue. The payoff has to be that you willingly choose to engage in the tremendous effort of change because you want more for yourself. You want to know that you value yourself so much you can stand with trembling legs and say, "no more" to old beliefs and behaviors. You want to know that you can make new choices that bring yourself greater empowerment and love.

Goals are set specifically to counter old patterns, behaviors, and survival strategies. You want to challenge those limiting beliefs so that one by one you can shed them and build your life on a new, confident foundation. Compelling reasons are how you are able to face fearful beliefs and say, "This may be the most difficult thing I ever do, but I will do it because I am stronger than I realize."

The reason behind the reason is the compelling answer to the questions, "Why do I want my goal? What will I have once I obtain what I want?" Suppose you wake up tomorrow and you have achieved everything you want to achieve with your goal. You have attained success. What would your success look like? What problems are solved and what is different now about your life?

- How do you feel in your body?

- What is different about your relationships?

- How do you feel when you get up in the morning?

- How is your eating different?

- What does your body look like, and how does that alter your life?

- What do you do during your day that you did not do before?

- What activities are you now engaged in?

- What strengths, talents, and feelings are present that were unavailable before you achieved your goal?

- What do you look like in those situations that used to be a problem?

- How do you think about those things that used to be a problem?

These questions offer a powerful frame for helping you establish your own goals and for uncovering your compelling reason to want change. Take your time describing your new life. Address the following areas of your life and write down the vision of your successful life.

- Eating

- Physical activity

- How you prioritize your time

- Play and relaxation

- Hobbies

- Body image

- Self-Acceptance

- Confidence

- Self-respect

- Relationships

- Interest in your life

- Assertiveness

- Emotions

- Self-care

- Medication

Your compelling reason is all about the personal values you wish to bring more fully into your life. What will your life look like once you achieve your goal? Using the above questions, describe your new life. Include how you are acting, feeling, and thinking in that new life:

_____

_____

_____

_____

_____

_____

_____

_____

_____

_____

_____

_____

_____

Goals that aim to fix a problem almost always miss the mark, while goals that aim to create a better life tend to succeed. If you accomplish your goal (you lose weight) without learning the deeper meaning of the behaviors that led you to the initial problem, it is unlikely to be a permanent fix. Why? The original beliefs and thought patterns remain unchanged. You set your goal not only to have the outcome but also to discover that you deserve to give yourself a happy life. Achieving your compelling reason is your main objective, and losing weight is a natural secondary outcome.

Your underlying compelling reason must become the focus of your attention, far more than simply losing weight or controlling your eating behaviors. In fact, this greater journey of identifying and pursuing your compelling reason will be so inspiring and life-altering, that even if you fail to achieve your purpose, you would endure weight issues all over again simply to obtain the higher level of self-empowerment and joy you need and want. In simpler words, if you fail to reach the outcome of your compelling reason, you may very well regain weight to give yourself another chance to have what you most want. The strength or confidence you gain from this journey is something that must be present for you to move more decisively into your life's purpose and joy.

A few examples of compelling reasons may include the ability to do the following:

- Build confidence, self-esteem, and strength from the inside.

- Discover you are capable of much more than you believe yourself to be.

- Stop feeling sorry for yourself.

- Stop waiting for someone else to heal or fix you.

- Put your needs first and take the steps needed to make your desires a reality.

- Spend your days doing what matters most, being focused on your passions and well-being.

- Feel more alive and vibrant because you are moving in a direction that gives you purpose.

- Let go of the past, forgive, and let go of your suffering.

- Allow your self to deal effectively with authority.

- Increase your tolerance for frustration during difficult circumstances.

- Be more naturally assertive.

- Handle criticism or confrontations more positively.

- Help your self develop a sense of belonging, comfort, and safety in the world.

- Let your self give and receive friendliness, care, and love.

- Allow your self to enjoy recreation and pleasure.

- Experience a deeper sense of comfort and peace.

- Learn to appreciate yourself and be proud of your choices.

- Free your sense of humor and ability to laugh at yourself.

- Let go of the need for approval from others.

- Gain a reasonable sense of independence and self-reliance.

A compelling reason is the secret ingredient that moves you from a state of inertia into action. It provides the burning desire to get out of the comfort zone even though it would be easier to stay. It is the driving motivational force to adopt an attitude of change. A compelling reason provides the impetus needed to stand back up after each failure. A compelling reason helps you overcome your own objections and excuses.

When you set a goal, you are going to have to make choices that you are not used to making. You may even set yourself apart from others in opting differently. You might get up at five a.m. because that is the only available hour to devote to exercise. You might choose a vegetable platter while your family is indulging in chicken fried steak with biscuits and gravy. As you become more involved in your own important pursuits, you might become less involved in other people's lives. New assertiveness skills might lead you to behave differently with certain people in your life. You will make these choices not just once but day after day until you have a successful outcome. Is it fair? Maybe not, but fair is not the point. The point is that you want something for *yourself*. Moreover, you want to know that you possess *within yourself* the quality to make that something happen.

The secret to setting effective goals is spending more explorative and creative time on the front end of goal setting. Discovering the reason behind your behavior is the one step most people would wish to skip altogether. Yet, without consciously knowing your compelling reason, it is difficult, if not impossible, to stay on track when times get tough. Take the time to complete the following exercise—even if completing it takes multiple attempts. You will find that the time and effort you invest on this activity will pay off in the future. Once you have constructed your compelling reason, display it somewhere prominent. Look at it often and remind yourself repeatedly why you want what you want.

How to Discover Your Underlying Motivation in About 20 Minutes

Your compelling reasons are about defining what you value in life and then using those values to guide your journey. It is a definition of who you are, what you stand for, and what is important to you. Knowing your underlying motivation helps keep you focused on your priorities in life and the goals you have for yourself. It gives you a chance to start over and make different choices. It gives you clear direction, and you are less likely to take the easy way out or accept short-term gains at the expense of your long-term goals. You make good decisions and quickly know which choices support you and which do not. You live with integrity, become a whole person, and make choices that allow you to be true to your self. Compelling values may include the following:

- Integrity—Giving yourself straightforward advice based solely on your desire to succeed

- Trust—Following through on your word to yourself

- Caring—Nurturing yourself in ways that lead to your success

- Respect—Gaining a sense of increased personal importance

- Continual Learning—Gaining increased ability to discover new solutions to old problems

- Commitment—Knowing your goal is important to you, and you will stick with it

- Passion—Finding new ways to get excited about your daily life and your long-term plans

- Optimism—Setting out to discover that you can indeed be successful in any area of life you choose to focus on

Your compelling reasons are the answers to why you want to stop your eating behaviors or lose weight. What inner strengths, talents, or personality traits will you unearth? What fear do you want to release or move past? What is the real reason you are making a goal?

Your life has purpose and value! You are setting your goal not to make yourself better in someone else's eyes but because achieving your goal is important to uncovering some aspect of yourself that you need to lead a happier, more fulfilled, or more confident life. It is time to go beneath the surface reasons of your goal and discover the real reasons you are about to embark on this life-changing journey.

Here is the exercise:

1. Use a piece of paper and write on top, "What is my compelling reason to have the outcome of my goal?"

2. Write an answer—any answer—even if it seems nonsensical. It does not have to be a complete sentence or even a meaningful answer. Just write down what first comes to mind. Take a moment, breathe deeply, clear your mind, and ask yourself:

   - What is this all about?

   - Why is this important?

   - What does this relate to?

   - What is at the heart of this issue?

   - What is important that I have not said yet?

Notice how you feel in your body, mind, and emotions. Notice what you have not yet thought, said, or written. Take another deep breath, wait a moment for your next thought to arise, and once again write down your answer to the question, "What is my compelling reason to have the outcome of my goal?"

3. Repeat step 2 and write your next compelling reason. Again, pause, breathe, reflect, and ask yourself what is important or meaningful to you about this reason.

- What is this all about?

- Why is this important?

- What does this relate to?

- What is at the heart of this issue?

- What is important that I have not said yet?

4. Repeat the process until you write the answer that makes you cry. This is your compelling reason.

That is it. This exercise usually takes 15–20 minutes in order to clear your head of all the clutter and the superficial reasons. Those first answers have merit, but they are not the true reason you are setting out to change your life. When the compelling reason finally arrives, it will feel like it is coming to you from a different source entirely.

For some people, this exercise might take longer than twenty minutes. In fact, it might require multiple attempts. However, if you persist, you will end up with an answer that you know is real. That answer will help you keep your purpose, will, and determination. At some point during this exercise, you may want to quit. You may feel the urge to get up and make an excuse to do something else. You may feel irritated, impatient, and expect the process to fail. That is great! It means you are taking this exercise seriously and getting closer to your compelling reason. Take a breath, move past this resistance, and keep writing. The feeling of resistance will eventually pass.

You may also discover a few answers that give you a mini-surge of emotion, but they do not quite make you cry; that means that you are very close, but not quite there. Highlight those answers as you go along. While each reflects a piece of your purpose, individually they are not complete. Keep going. You may write 50, 100, 200, or more answers before you finally get your compelling reason. Just keep relaxing, contemplating, and writing until you find it. Your efforts will reward you well in your coming journey.

Write down your core compelling motivation:

Compelling reason: _____

"To me, success means . . ." _____

_____

_____

_____

_____

Chapter Four

Illuminate Your Ideal Future

—Constructive Complaining—

Before you can attempt to meet your goals, you have to know what they are. However, how do you know clearly and specifically what you want? Certainly, you may have an idea of what you want. You want to end your eating behavior or lose weight. However, that is an ambiguous goal stating what you want to move away from, but not identifying in simple and specific terms your ideal outcome. As you have already seen, your deepest desire is not only to end an eating behavior but to advance matters of core importance.

If you are like many people, you have a much clearer picture of what you do not want in your life than what you do want. You know when you feel sad, angry, dissatisfied, or upset that something is wrong. You know when you are discouraged, when you have thought patterns you want to change, actions you want to discontinue, and emotions you would like to minimize. You can easily identify that you do not want to feel stressed, depressed, or controlled by food. Allowing yourself to complain about what is wrong in your life is actually a good entrance into pinpointing your most wanted outcomes.

Complaining about what is wrong with your life provides a great starting position. However, you cannot just think and dwell internally on everything that is wrong. In addition, venting your frustrations to another person might help you release steam, but just dumping your problems on someone else will not create change in your life. It is most helpful if you utilize your grievances as a way to see them, get them out in the open, identify that you want resolution, and then take responsibility to do something about them. One way to do this is to write down your woes and challenges.

As you write down your complaints, remind yourself that all feelings are a valuable source of information. Yes, some emotions feel pleasurable while others are seemingly unbearable; however, there are no "good" feelings or "bad" feelings. They are all information provided from you and given to you. Emotions, stress, and worry can tell you where you feel disempowered, where you believe yourself to be at risk, or where you believe yourself unable to effect change. Your complaints contain information about what is true for you in this moment. They inform you of the relationship you currently have with your self, with your body, and with your life. They can tell you where you have shut down from love or where you have beliefs of limitation, doubt, or unworthiness. When you complain and take notice of your complaints, you put a voice to what you believe about the world and your place in it.

Listen to your emotions and your inner thoughts and let loose. Do not hold back! Make a list of what really irritates you about having to face your challenge and having to set goals. What disgusts you about your body? What do you hate about food? What do you despise about being you? What situations cause you stress, grief, pain, or frustration? Write down everything you dislike about your life, yourself, your body, and the way you eat. Put down on paper anything that is making your life miserable. Write down all those things you think you *should* be doing but you know you do not want to do. Here is an example to get you started:

This is not fair that I have to work on this problem. It is just food and I should be able to handle something so simple on my own. I hate that my desire for comfort from food is greater than my desire for the delayed gratification of losing weight. I hate that I have to deal with this problem at all. I hate myself for wanting to eat the food. I do not want this

constant inner struggle. I do not want to be thinking all the time about what to eat, what

not to eat, and when to eat. I do not want to be this stressed about the money I spend on

food and being broke all the time because of it. I do not want to be fat, but at the same

time I do not have the energy to do anything about it. Besides, what is the use of trying

to overcome this issue one more time? I will just fail again.

If, suddenly, you have encountered writer's block and cannot seem to get your complaints down onto paper, here is an alternate but equally revealing exercise: Wait until a time when you have used food to deal with life or your emotions, and then go to a mirror with a tape recorder. Take a long look at yourself, remember the choice you just made with food, turn on the tape, and start talking about your life, your body, and your behaviors. Say all the things you usually think inside your head, but this time speak them out loud. I imagine your words will be flying! If not, take off your clothes in front of the mirror and see what happens.

When you are ready, listen to the tape and transcribe your grievances and bellyaches onto paper. It is most helpful to see your complaints out in the open, out in front of you. Your complaints are important because they contain the truth of what you currently feel or believe. When you look at your complaints with non-judgmental eyes, you can easily identify your innermost desires and needs. Typically, what you want is usually the exact opposite of the situations, actions, thoughts, and feelings that you do not want.

What I Don't Want Worksheet

Turn Your Complaints into Assets

Now that you have taken the time to clarify what you do not want, the task of identifying your goal is halfway complete. You have a much clearer sense of what you do not want, what does not feel good, or where you believe yourself to be disempowered. Complaining and writing it down on paper allowed you to give voice to your emotions. You gained a sense of what you want to move *away from*. But, do not stop here! Complaining by itself is not going to allow for any improvement in your life. If you just complain, you will most likely end up obsessing about your undesirable situation or feeling more frustrated or helpless. To illustrate this point let us play a game for a moment. Read the following paragraph, then close your eyes, review the words, and be aware of your thoughts:

Do NOT see a large pink elephant in a circus ring. Do NOT see a cute, tiny blue mouse scampering around the left front foot of the pink elephant. Do NOT listen to the tinkling bell jingling from the collar around the neck of the blue mouse.

Before reading further, stop and notice what your mind did with the above instructions. It is impossible to not see, feel, or hear some version of the pink elephant and blue mouse story. Your mind had to create some kind of vision that may have included an image, sound, or feeling. Then, in one form or another, your mind had to follow your directions about NOT seeing or hearing the image. Your mind somehow dismissed the image. First, your mind creates the image and then the image fades away, is wiped out, or is released.

Now, read the pink elephant paragraph again, and notice exactly how your mind deals with the instructions to not do something. Be aware of what you actually visualize or imagine, and then be aware of what you do to dismiss the image. Because no one provided further instruction on what to focus on instead of this image, your mind had to release the image but could not move onto something different. How does you mind deal with an instruction not to do something? What does your mind do when you finally release this thought? Does it create a blank? Does it cause a feeling of confusion or even an illusion of failure?

When you hear yourself saying, "I do not want to binge anymore," or, "I do not want to feel so depressed and overwhelmed," pause for a moment and notice what happens in your mind, thoughts, and emotions. Just like in the example above, you gave your mind a specific instruction of what you did not want it to do. Because of how your mind works, this type of instruction can only lead your mind to create a vision, image, or feeling of the experience you do not want and then let go of that image.

Consider another example where you tell yourself, "I want to lose weight." With that focus, your mind dwells on what you want to *lose* not what you want to *gain*. Focusing on the life you do not want can move you away from something, but it cannot move you toward a specific objective. Successful outcomes begin when you learn to set your sights on what you desire and the benefits that come along with that desire.

Now that you have defined what you want to move away from, it is time to take the next step. It is easy to flip around what you do not want in order to identify more clearly what you do want. For example:

- "I do not want to feel stressed," becomes: "I want to feel relaxed in my body, breathe more deeply, and use my inner voice to support myself when I am at work, around people, or at home."

- "I do not want to struggle with my weight," becomes: "I want a loving partnership with my body and the ability to positively motivate myself to create a 180-pound body that I enjoy living in."

- "I do not want to engage in emotional eating," becomes: "I want to feel more calm and confident in my own body, be able to breathe through my emotions, find my center, and then make self-supporting choices."

- "I do not want to be out of control with food," becomes: "I want to eat in a way that is satisfying and fulfilling, listening to my body's cues of enjoyment and satiety."

- "I do not want to be stuck with this eating habit," becomes: "I want to feel the sense of empowerment that will come from knowing I can make eating decisions that feel good in my body."

Recall the example above, which read:

This is not fair that I have to work on this problem. It is just food, and I should be able to handle something so simple on my own. I hate that my desire for comfort from food is greater than my desire for the delayed gratification of losing weight. I hate that I have to deal with this problem at all. I hate myself for wanting to eat the food. I do not want this constant inner struggle. I do not want to be thinking all the time about what to eat, what not to eat, and when to eat. I do not want to be this stressed about the money I spend on food and about being broke all the time because of it. I do not want to be fat, but at the same time I do not have the energy to do anything about it. Besides, what is the use of trying to overcome this issue one more time? I will just fail again.

In this example, many limiting beliefs and thoughts are identified. This person believes that the situation is not fair, that it should be simple to create change, and that something is wrong because she or he cannot figure it out. This individual feels a lack of willpower and therefore feels helpless in the face of the challenge. From this example, we can easily see the foundations of a successful goal if we turn around the complaints into a forward-reaching direction. We could turn this complaint session around 180 degrees and write:

It may not be fair that I have to work on this problem, but I accept that this is my challenge to overcome and that my challenges are meaningful. I can see that my emotions, inner turmoil, and food behaviors are a result of wanting something much grander for myself. This is a good thing, and it shows that I have love for myself. The roots of this issue go deeper than just losing weight, and therefore the solution is not as simplistic as counting calories. I feel better seeing the bigger picture, and I want more of this bal-anced perspective. I am in the process of gaining greater appreciation for my life and my body. It is now obvious to me that I have a great ability to maintain attention and focus. Instead of trying to get rid of that part of me, I can use that talent to focus on desires and actions that bring me greater joy. As I do so, I eliminate my mind's preoccupation with food. Naturally, I will spend less money on food. I want to weigh 180 pounds. I want to believe in my ability to succeed and have what I want. And I want to feel energetic.

Now, take a long look at the list of complaints you wrote down earlier. Imagine that you are looking at them from a higher perspective. Instead of being down-in-the-trenches and engulfed in emotions and judgment, climb to the mountaintop and see your situation from a new vantage point. Within your complaints are the raw ingredients of what you want for yourself and for your life. Turn your complaints around 180 degrees; and, maybe for the first time ever, see clearly what you do want!

Identify What I Do Want Worksheet

Go back to the previous exercise and flip what you do not want to feel, think, or experience around 180 degrees. Make sure you say what you want, the way that you want it—not the way you do not want it but the way you want it. Write down the experience that you want to live, breathe, and experience.

_____

_____

_____

_____

_____

_____

Chapter Five

Knowing What You Want—And Getting It!

—Generate a Living, Breathing, Inspired Plan—

When most people attempt to achieve a goal, especially a weight loss goal, they make a big mistake. They approach the day-to-day action process from a purely logical perspective—meaning that they spend their efforts trying to fix the problem. Yet, as you know, losing weight and keeping it off requires more than portion control and ample amounts of exercise. It requires using your mind, body, and spirit in fresh ways.

How often have you heard yourself say you wanted to lose weight and then, following logic, you simply tighten your grip on your food intake? You find a plan, follow the steps, and do everything right. Utilizing self-control and willpower, you restrict what you eat. It works for a while. However, soon you find yourself obsessing about what you can eat, what you cannot eat, when you can eat, and how many calories are in each food serving. Ultimately, you either fail to achieve the outcome or fail to maintain the outcome. As a result, you feel frustrated. You might even begin to believe that either something is wrong with you or that your situation is hopeless.

Even though restricting caloric intake seems to make sense, it tends to focus your energy on the problem and not the solution. Instead of developing new relationships with future hopes, you are trapped trying to fix the relationship with a worn-out, undesirable way of thinking and acting. Traditional weight loss efforts often direct attention to the problem, thereby blocking the creative energy and inspiration needed to develop a new partnership with life and yourself.

The biggest mistake people make when setting weight goals is by making an issue out of weight loss. Of course you want to lose weight! That *will* happen but not without addressing the underlying desire to improve your emotional, spiritual, and physical life. You want to lose weight because you are feeling lonely, lacking confidence, or feeling out-of-control, uninspired, depressed, anxious, or doubtful. Simply eliminating excess pounds will not create the psychological reality that you desire. If you do end up losing the weight, you will still lack social connection, confidence, or greater happiness. A successful plan has to create a new way of believing, thinking, and acting.

Your journey is not about the strict following of rules or pre-designed diets, it is about finding your balance between inspiration and logic. It is about being inflexible with your desires but flexible with your approach. The process should develop a better life, not just a better figure. By engaging in the process of change, you discover that you can choose what you want in life and that you do indeed have the inner capability to make that life happen. You could use force to get what you want, but that would leave you feeling unsatisfied. Instead, having goals shows you a new way of living life. They show you how to use the duel qualities of inspiration and logic to envision a new possibility, breathe life into your idea, and then make your idea physically tangible. Your benefits to achieving this balance include identifying the following:

- Which limiting beliefs are holding you back—and how to move beyond them into success.

- What your version of a successful life would look like and feel like.

- How to shift your focus from temporary pleasure to the fulfillment of an authentic life.

- How to ignite inner passion and bring purpose and meaning back into your life.

- How to develop effective self-leadership skills and work smarter, not harder, to achieve your outcome.

- How to tap into your creative spirit and go to the heart of successful living.

- How to develop internal support, positive motivation, and greater self-love.

Traditional goal setting will be weighty and limited if you rely predominantly on logic or rules to fix the problem. Logic without inspiration forces you to doggedly strive for success but never feel satisfied in the process. Your goal process is so much more than just a means to an end. It is a journey allowing you to develop deeper inner peace combined with energetic involvement in your life. Your new approach to solving your food or weight challenge: allow your inspiration to get involved by suggesting creative solutions, and *then* utilize logic to move forward.

The Strengths of Logic

It is important to understand how to harness the power of logic so that you may employ its strengths to work for you instead of inadvertently allowing it to hamper your efforts. *Logic* is the brilliant, intellectual, masculine aspect of you. This quality within you has the amazing ability to take action and move forward, getting things done. Its strengths include the ability to be linear, analytical, and methodical. It implements step-by-step sequential actions—first-things-first and then second-things-second. Logic also has the ability to pay attention to detail. It is unemotional and can do what needs to be done, when it needs to be done. Logic is the part of you that can provide a careful assessment of your goal and outline your strengths, weaknesses, opportunities, and potential threats.

Logic has the ability to work from knowledge gained from **past** experiences and apply that wisdom to **present** situations. In comparison, inspiration is the part of you that works with the **future**. Logic allows you to look back and benefit from reflection. It can determine what has or has not worked previously. If it did not work last time, it is not going to work this time, unless modifications are implemented. Using these abilities, logic can create a solid foundation for success. Once that groundwork is in place, logic then helps you manage time, stay focused on your goal, and complete tasks.

Logic traits include the following:

- Linear and sequential, one step at a time

- Organizational

- Rational

- Detail-oriented

- Practical and realistic

- Analytical

- Objective

- Literal and functional

- Time oriented

The strengths of logic are many, yet when logic overpowers inspiration, your goal journey can be rigid and stressful. The unemotional nature of logic excludes necessary feelings such as hope of a better future, faith in good things to come, and perseverance due to love of self. Logic is about reason, rationality, and rule-following. In addition, your analytical side is skeptical of innovation. Therefore, if you have always believed that dieting is the way to lose weight then, despite past diet failures, you will continue to seek the *right* diet. This function of logic explains the tendency to try diet after diet and an unwillingness to look in new directions for inventive solutions.

Logic sees things as right or wrong, black or white, and good or bad. Therefore, when one action fails, logic will tell you that the entire goal must be unachievable. Moreover, because logic deals only with the past and present, it is unable to help you visualize a future different from the present. When an action fails to achieve a predicted outcome, logic demands that you examine the microcosm of the failure rather than the whole picture. With your analytical side in control, it is easy to see why you often feel you wasted an entire day or week because of one splurge or overeating episode.

Another drawback of relying heavily on logic alone is that it will demand that you try to "fix" the problem. The logical mind begins to fight the problem, think about it, and obsess over it. It will try to stop the action of overeating *without* addressing important underlying concerns. For example, you might say to yourself, "My purpose for eating differently is to weigh less." However, is that your real purpose? Is that what is going to keep you motivated? Every goal comes down to a *feeling* that you want to expand. You might want to feel better about yourself, develop more confidence, or enlarge your self-worth. Logic does not deal with emotion. Therefore, using logic alone will drive you to change your pattern of consumption without addressing your need to improve how you feel about life, yourself, or food right now. It is difficult, if not impossible, to trust your body to make the right choices for yourself in the moment or to rely on bodily wisdom, with logic in complete control. Logic cannot:

- Have compassion for your situation or your challenges.

- Discover creative ways to control your response to hunger.

- Seek innovative ways to deal with nighttime or boredom eating.

- Comfort you spiritually or emotionally.

- Understand how to relieve stress without food.

- See the big picture when crises and failures occur.

- Handle obstacles without wanting to give up.

- Soothe and comfort without food.

- See the worth or value of emotions.

We do not need to abandon logic but instead learn better ways of how and when to apply it. Ways to utilize the strengths of a logical approach include analyzing the past and present, defining the problem, and clarifying the desired outcome. Logic allows you to become aware of your own habits, desires, and motivations. It can aid in determining feasibility, potential obstacles, and a reasonable time frame. Logic provides a core of practicality to all you do; in fact, it allows you to read and complete this workbook! To focus your logical skills on your goal, answer the following questions:

- What exactly is the problem?

- How often does the problem occur?

- What precedes the problem?

- Have I tried to resolve this problem before, and what was the result?

- What has worked in the past?

- What has not worked in the past?

- Has anybody else tried to solve a similar problem?

Utilize logic to help you evaluate past actions and gather insights about what has and has not worked previously.

_____

_____

_____

_____

_____

_____

_____

_____

_____

The Strengths of Inspiration

While your logic is responsible for the important tasks of reviewing the past, applying past successful results to current strategies, and taking action, your creative, inspirational aspect provides the necessary balance of encouragement and imaginative insight. Your creative intelligence processes information differently than your logical intelligence. Inspiration can peer into the future and see life as it could be. It examines the "big picture" and seeks to determine the spatial relationship of all the parts as they relate to the whole. It is not concerned with following the rules and instead relies on intuition and imagination to provide a sense of what action is right for each moment.

Inspiration develops once you understand your compelling reason for wanting change. Do you want more confidence, more passion, more love for yourself? If you know what you want, you can focus on actions that create this "more" in your life. Your inspiration can speak to you and design creative solutions. It seeks out opportunities and finds them!

Inspiration is the part of you that dreams of wonderful outcomes. It is your ability to see a future beyond your current experiences. It is your feminine aspect, full of creativity, resourcefulness, intuition, and emotions. It is your creative genius, allowing unforeseen opportunities to develop. Inspiration intuitively knows what action or effort is most important to the journey at each step.

Inspiration is imaginative and future-focused. While logic can only consider the past and work in the present, inspiration is able to focus on the master plan. Inspiration allows you to look forward to a life in which you have success, empowerment, and joy. It helps you move away from the present problem and examine your situation from a future perspective. Inspiration can help you imagine yourself living new potentials, thereby providing hope for success.

Inspiration builds a bridge between the life you are now living and the life you desire. It is the spiritual and mystical aspect of the goal, linking unique talents, strengths, and purpose with your desired outcome. It is inspiration that stirs passion! It breathes life into the journey and creates an atmosphere of overall enthusiasm and adventure. Instead of taking each step with drudgery, inspiration provides meaning to actions and infuses each step with these qualities:

- Life-energy

- Creative spirit

- New perspective and the ability to dream

- A sense of purpose

- Compassion for the journey and hope for success

- New ideas, concepts, or associations

- Courage

- Loving-kindness

- Ability to visualize solutions

- A relationship with your goal

- Tolerance for chance, synchronicity, and following gut feelings

- Acceptance of failure as a temporary situation

This bridge of inspiration is necessary to allow you to move beyond survival and stress behaviors into the ability to activate empowered, self-loving aspects of yourself. Inspiration is the factor that alters thought patterns away from self-criticism to acknowledgement of effort and success. Inspiration connects the current you with greater potentials and possibilities. Inspiration is the love that you are and the creative ideas that you have for yourself.

As we can see, the strengths of inspiration are many. However, there are also weaknesses associated with predominantly relying on inspiration. Inspiration is the limitless world of dreams and possibilities. Yet logic must bring those ideas to reality by taking action. Inspiration tends to involve ideas that are often complex and difficult to articulate. However, logic must organize these concepts into actionable form. Inspiration is often intuitive and inwardly aware of many conflicting emotions. Logic organizes inspired thoughts into a practical method, allowing you to take action and move forward despite difficult emotions.

To get the most out of your inspirational abilities, answer the following questions:

- What does the big picture look like? What do I want to have, live, and feel?

- What actions will elicit excitement and passion?

- How can I make my actions more rewarding, more creative, or more exciting?

- What steps will I take to remain focused on the bigger picture?

- What will I do to remain focused on the compelling reason for seeking change?

- What actions strengthen and empower?

- What actions encourage?

- What actions increase my ability to respect, accept, recognize, and love my body, self, and life?

- What actions expand my self-leadership qualities of courage, trust, faith, respect, enthusiasm, curiosity, delight, and caring?

- What actions help me connect with life-enhancing energy?

- How will I channel creative energy into the process of attaining this goal?

List any creative or inspirational ideas that may be stirring within you now:

_____

_____

_____

_____

_____

_____

_____

_____

_____

_____

The Fusion of Logic and Inspiration Equals Inspired Action

Many people who have difficulty meeting their goals and objectives have an imbalance between logic and inspiration. The two parts of the mind seem to be at war with one another. Indeed, a balanced masculine/feminine mind-relationship is not inherent. It is something that develops with practice. Think of this connection as a muscle—the more you exercise it, the stronger it becomes!

The two aspects of your mind have different strengths, and to some extent, we could say that these qualities are opposite. Instead of thinking of them as conflicting, consider them dual strengths that work best when they achieve harmonious coexistence. Each is ineffective without the balance of the other. Only the combination of logic and inspiration creates loving self-leadership, long-term self-initiative, and fulfilling success.

A satisfying and successful adventure occurs as you develop a partnership between the intuitive, creative, inspirational side of your personality and your highly action-oriented logical side. Inspiration is the part of you that is filled with hope and a vision of life as it could be. It dreams wonderful outcomes and allows you to see a future beyond your current experience. It is also your ability to know intuitively which action is right for right now. Inspiration provides the action idea that will expand your ability to feel better, more confident, or more empowered today as it relates to your overall goal. If one action fails to produce the desired result, inspiration offers perspective and generates new possibilities. Inspiration allows for experimentation, flexibility, and openness to new ideas. It brings curiosity, enthusiasm, energy, playfulness, and a sense of comfort with change.

Logic is the part of you that converts your inspiration into a practical, today action step. It moves beyond emotional resistance and conflict, focuses your attention on the present, concentrates your efforts using commitment and persistence, and provides the capacity for hard work. One of the main strengths of logic is that it compels action. As a result, it is wise to allow logic to work for you only after you *first* allow your inspiration to imagine the desired result. Allow inspiration to help you visualize the wholeness of the life you want to live. Allow inspiration to show you how you want to think, feel, and act in your new life. Allow inspiration to offer innovative solutions. *Then,* and *only* then, allow logic to act on these ideas.

Inspired actions come from an internal nudge. Learn to pay attention to your hunches. For example, ask yourself, "Which action will I take *today*?" Listen for your answer. Be sure to take time to listen to your creative voice. Inspiration is not necessarily logical, rational, or something that you "should" be doing. Instead, it is an action that you know, inside of yourself, is the correct one for you now. An inspired action is the action that gets you moving in the right direction, raises your energy levels, and gets you personally involved in applying innovative solutions to old problems.

Search within and notice that you already know if you will follow through with your action or not. If you know that the action you chose is not one that will lead to success, choose again. Selecting an action that taxes your current resources, capabilities, or time constraints is self-sabotage. Your entire goal exists because of your desire to feel better, so opt for actions that you can commit to attaining. If you complete your specific action, you will feel good right away. You will reinforce your growing belief that you can have what you want, that the change you desire is possible. By contrast, if you choose an action and do not follow through, you immediately feel bad, lose energy and motivation, and maintain old, limiting belief systems.

Establish balance between logic and inspiration by looking at your overall "big picture" goal and then by choosing an inspired action for today. Use logic to determine if you will follow through with that action. If you already know that you will not reach completion, choose another action. By combining inspiration and logic in this new order you can bring your future vision into today *and* feel better right now. While your big picture is solid and unchanging, your inspired actions are generally determined each day. They are highly flexible, intuitive, perceptive, and change readily with the benefit of trial and error. This fusion between logic and inspiration provides you with a sense of stability and direction but also allows you to enjoy the steps of your journey!

The SMARTEST Goal Setting Techniques

Now that you understand the importance of bringing life, breath, and heart to your journey, it is time to take advantage of the proven science of goal setting! Turn your *What I Do Want* list from above into a SMART goal. The word SMART is an acronym for breaking your goals down into a specific, motivational, attainable, realistic approach, with a targeted completion date. Instead of reinventing the wheel, learn from the wisdom of others and create a personal roadmap to success with the help of this invaluable resource.

S—Specific	Know exactly what you want.
M—Measurable	Make measurable steps of progress.
A—Achievable	Set challenging goals that are within your reach.
R—Relevant	Have goals that bring about a rewarding feeling.
T—Timely	Set a definable amount of time to reach the goal.

Make It SPECIFIC

To understand how the SMART system works, let us begin with a simple example.

If I were to make the statement, "I will lose weight," is this goal a SMART goal?

No, it is not SPECIFIC or detailed enough.

To be specific, your goal must answer the what, why, and how questions.

- What are you moving toward?

- Why is this important to have or do right now?

- What inner qualities or strengths will you develop during the process of attaining your goal?

- How will you feel both during the actual process of attaining your goal and afterwards?

Your specific goals might read:

- I am now in the process of achieving my goal to end binge eating by July 5th.

- I will take at least two positive daily actions everyday until I reach my target.

- At the end of each day, I will recognize my efforts and successes by writing them down. These steps will help me feel good about myself.

- I will look in the mirror each day and see myself as confident, worthy, and full of self-love.

- Putting effort into my goal will help me feel empowered, proud, peaceful, and satisfied.

Your overall goal is your big picture. It is solid and gives you something to believe in, to spend your energy and efforts on, and to guide your decisions. Once your big-picture goal is in place it tends to be unchanging, and thereby gives you strength.

How Do You Know if You Are Achieving Success? Can You MEASURE It?

Measurable action steps are a combination of creative, inspired thought and practical, logical application. They are highly flexible. Each time you take a step, you will measure your progress and evaluate the effectiveness of your action. Did your action bring new life? Increase motivation? Give a slightly greater sense of empowerment? Measurable steps are continuously updated, modified, or fine-tuned to allow consistent and positive forward movement.

State measurable actions in such language that allows an objective, not a subjective, determination of success. An action stated, "Today, I will try harder," is a subjective statement. Reword this statement into a specific action that you will take today. If you cannot measure your action, then you cannot see progress occurring. Choose a measurable action that seems right for right now.

Examples of measurable goals include the following statements:

- I will walk 10–30 minutes around my neighborhood at least three times a week.

- Three days a week, I will exchange morning doughnuts for fruit and a break with work friends.

- Four days a week, I will eat 3–5 servings of vegetables each day.

- I will write in my journal daily.

- I will set up a special calendar and mark on it every meal in which I engage in binge eating. I will give myself a star for every time I stop the behavior; this way I can see my ratio of success.

- I will take care of my body by walking in nature every week, breathing deeply and intentionally at least five times a day, getting a chair massage once every two weeks, and taking a bath—complete with candles and soothing music—once a week.

Is It ACHIEVABLE Yet Challenging?

People who set goals that are achievable yet challenging build their confidence at the same time. Having lofty aspirations is important; at the same time, your target must be realistic. You want a goal that is empowering, one that you are willing and able to reach. What you do not want is a goal that is so fantastical that it serves to de-motivate. When your goal is sensible and significant, you become far more motivated to fulfill your hopes.

A goal that reads, "I will never overeat again," is unrealistic. Many people occasionally overeat, and since you are in the habit of overeating, there is a chance you might eventually revert to the familiar pattern. An achievable yet challenging goal might read, "I will stop the habit of emotional eating within one year, and I will do so by learning one new self-soothing strategy each week."

Is It RELEVANT?

Your goals need a strong purpose behind them. The journey is going to be filled with challenges, and you need to have a powerful reason for wanting to move forward despite encountering difficulties. You have already uncovered your compelling reason, so defining relevance is now easy for you. Remember, it is not enough to state, "I want to overcome overeating." You have to know why you want put yourself through the effort this process will entail. What is the daily payoff and the end result? What do you truly care about having for yourself? What gets you so excited that you are willing to devote your energy and efforts to having what you want, no matter what?

In case you are still in the process of discovering your compelling reason, here are a few clues:

- Have you based your goals on what you think you should be doing, or did these goals originate from your deepest desires?

- What is the spark and purpose of your goals? Peace? Joy? Fulfillment? Meaning?

- Will the journey itself expand the love within you?

Slap It with a TIMELINE, for Goodness' Sake!

There is an old saying that says, "A goal without a deadline is just a wish." Having a defined timeline keeps you motivated. It gives you a clear target. When you do not set a time frame, the commitment is too vague and breeds procrastination. Without a time limit, there is no sense of urgency to start taking action now.

In this acronym, **T** also stands for tangible. Being able to see, hear, and feel your goal will greatly increase your success. Too often, goals are floating around in our minds. We do not take the time to personify them. We need to use as many senses as possible to awaken a powerful desire to achieve these goals. What would the physical experience of having your goal look like, sound like, and feel like?

Using SMART to Write Your Big Picture Vision

S—Specific	Know exactly what you want
M—Measurable	Make measurable steps of progress
A—Achievable	Set challenging goals that are within your reach
R—Relevant	Have goals that bring about a rewarding feeling
T—Timely	Set a definable amount of time to reach the goal

Goal # 1:

I want to be thin and never overeat again.

That example is a good start, but it is not a SMART goal. It lacks both effort and enthusiasm. This statement feels harsh, self-punishing, and unrealistic.

Goal #2:

Within ten months, I will lose sixty pounds by incorporating thirty minutes of cardiovascular exercise six days per week.

It is specific: sixty pounds

It is measurable: step on a scale or know a specific clothing size

It is action-oriented and achievable: thirty minutes, six days/week

It is realistic: about 1.5 pounds/week would equal sixty pounds in ten months

It is timed: in ten months

Technically, this certainly fits the SMART goal criteria, but it also does not sound like any fun. This plan of action meets the specifications of logic, but it does not account for your need to include creativity, passion, and inspiration. Without the balance of logic and spirit, the goal is bound to fail either right from the start or over the long haul.

Goal #3:

Within ten months, I will have a wonderful, new relationship with food, my body, and my life. I will gain the freedom to eat what I want in satisfying amounts. I will enjoy food and eating! To achieve this I will make new decisions and follow through with my promises to myself. Because of that, I will gain confidence in myself. I will show myself that I can have what I want and that my efforts do matter. I will practice daily deep breathing to cope with my stress. I will set aside the money I once used to pay for food and use it to buy comfortable, fashionable clothes at the end of each month. This will make my journey more enjoyable. Each meal provides a new opportunity to enjoy food, connect with my spirit, and create a comfortable physical experience. I will experiment with walking, yoga, swimming, Pilates, and bike riding to discover which type of movement feels energizing and enjoyable. I will engage in some type of enjoyable movement or activity a minimum of 20 minutes, four days out of seven. I have always wanted to paint but never allowed myself the time to engage in this activity. I will buy paint supplies, register in an art class, and paint Tuesday and Thursday evenings. By doing these actions, I give my mind something meaningful to think about which may alleviate my preoccupation with food and calories.

Now, that is an example of a SMART goal that balances logic with spirit! The goal is specific, meaningful, achievable, relevant, and has a timeline. In addition, there is a sense of excitement and growing life energy imbedded into the desire itself. The good feelings occur not only at the end but also at every step of the way. Yes, the goal will take work to achieve, and it will not always be easy, but this goal adds heart to the journey. Articulated and brought into plain view is the spirit of the goal, the energy of desire, and the power of self-determination to create a happy life.

SMART Goal Worksheet

State the goal in **SPECIFIC** terms.

What is the *overall goal* I want to accomplish? What do I want and why do I want it?

What skill, inner strength, or characteristic does this goal bring into my life?

_____

_____

_____

State the goal in **MEASUREABLE** terms.

How will I know when progress occurs?

_____

_____

_____

State the goal in **ACHIEVABLE** terms.

Balance big dreams with small aims that are achievable at this time.

_____

_____

_____

State the goal in **RELEVANT** terms.

What are my compelling reasons for accomplishing this goal? What will the process of

attaining this goal give me that I do not have now?

_____

_____

_____

State the goal in **TANGIBLE** terms with a **TIMELINE**.

When will I achieve my goal? What will I *see*, *hear*, and *feel* as I cultivate my desire?

_____

_____

_____

Write your SMART goal that satisfies both the mind and spirit:

_____

_____

_____

_____

_____

_____

_____

_____

_____

_____

_____

_____

_____

_____

_____

_____

_____

_____

_____

_____

Chapter Six

Take Charge of Your Life

—Change Is Possible—

Have you ever heard of the expression "getting up on the wrong side of the bed"? There was a time when I would wake up with a less than idyllic attitude. Every morning, I would awaken with a sense of anxiety and dread. It was awful. The worst part was my inability to identify the specific reason for these feelings. No matter how well my life was going, these feelings persisted.

Unconsciously, I learned to move away from this feeling by getting up so quickly that I would not have to notice it was there. The alarm would ring full blast. I would push the covers away, switch on the bright lights, and hit the shower running. Immediately embracing the day was a great plan of distraction that allowed me to bypass the uncomfortable feeling. For the most part, it was successful.

However, feelings do not go away, even if we do everything in our power to ignore, avoid, or suppress them. A distraction strategy is not the same as waking up delighted to be alive. One day, I decided to take matters into my own hands. I finally realized that the feeling of dread was not going to vanish with the passage of time. I wanted to wake up and have the first minutes of my day match the rest of the great life I had created. I wanted to wake up feeling safe, comfortable, and optimistic.

What does this have in common with your desire to end overeating? Everything!

Every single goal contains the underlying decision to increase empowerment and feel better. For a long time, your style of eating served you well. It is your distraction from an uncomfortable feeling. Your eating behaviors briefly calm, soothe, and distract you from a belief or emotion. Food itself can release powerful chemical and hormonal responses that create a sense of temporary well-being. Eating is one solution to cope with your emotions or situation.

Your method works in a similar way to my morning distraction plan. If you are now wanting to change things it is because you have reached a point in your life where distraction is not enough. My reason to create change was not *just* to end the frantic morning ritual, and your reason to create change is not *just* to eat differently or weigh less. Your compelling reason for change is to *feel* better from the inside out. For example, in addition to eating differently and weighing less you want to lift the burden of depression, feel the lightness of greater confidence, or deal more assertively with your life's challenges.

My compelling reason for undertaking this journey was that I wanted to create a different type of morning for myself. I wanted to know that I had the ability to take responsibility for my life and emotions at every point in my day. To achieve this, I identified what I did not want and what I wanted instead. In this case, I did not want to wake up in the morning feeling bad, and I did not want to continue utilizing my distraction strategies. Rather, I wanted to feel the same overall level of safety and comfort in the morning that I felt throughout the rest of the day.

I began to go through the logical process of defining what actions I could take to bring this about. This included asking the logical questions and gathering data, as follows:

- What is the problem? *Waking up sad.*

- How often does it happen? *Every morning.*

- What have I done in the past? *Distracted myself with a frantic morning routine.*

- Has it worked? *Yes, but even years of doing this has not erased the feeling or created morning comfort.*

- Is it possible to change the way I feel in the morning? *I do not know the answer. Based on past experience the answer is no, based on hopeful inspiration the answer is yes.*

- Are there any examples of being able to do this? *Perhaps, but none that I am aware of at the present time.*

- What specific actions did other people take to achieve success? *I am unaware of other people's strategy or action steps for success with this particular issue.*

- What could I do differently right now? *There are no logical answers based on my experiences.*

- What is the "right" step? *Again, I see no logical first step.*

In this particular goal, I had an advantage that you do not have. Unlike with the weight loss industry, I found no sleek packages promising to help me find tranquility in the morning. There were no "joy" diets or anxiety-erasing meal plans. There was no expansive World Wide Web offering an array of self-help programs. In retrospect, it was to my benefit that I had to look within and discover my own strengths to accomplish change. This allowed me to forego relying solely on logic or giving my power to something or someone outside of myself. Since there was no obvious place to turn and logic provided no insight, I had to trust in my own creativity and perseverance.

I began to experiment with different potential solutions, taking it one step at a time. This new balance between logic and inspiration allowed me to stop playing the victim and urged me into inspired action. While logic alone would have focused on fixing the problem, inspiration took a different direction. Instead of fighting to eliminate the current reality, I focused on generating a future reality that included greater comfort.

Could I do it? Was it possible to wake up feeling considerably better? I did not know the answer but decided I was willing to try. So what would be the first step? Again, I did not know. However, it seemed reasonable to read inspirational books and articles, gathering evidence that it is possible for any individual to create a more desirable emotional state. Reading the proof of other people's success provided initial optimism and motivation.

Next, I bought a journal and put it next to my bed. Now, instead of hiding from the feeling I would confront reality. Every morning for two weeks I woke up, and before even getting out of bed, I wrote. I described my emotions in detail, observed how they affected my physical body, and explained how I felt about these sensations. Instead of running away from the problem, I sat with it and allowed the heaviness and sense of dread to have a voice. By encouraging a sense of curiosity about my situation, I began to honor my body and myself, giving expression to the feeling I had so long resisted.

Because I did not know what the next step should be, I experimented with several alternatives to create a more inviting bedroom atmosphere. I bought a new alarm clock that played soothing music instead of a shrill alarm. That was certainly better on my ears but seemed to have little effect on my mood. Next, instead of jumping up into the day, I decided to lounge in bed for ten minutes snuggling with my cat. The cat idea added warmth and gentleness to my morning, but it did not erase the anxiety. Next, I went to the Hallmark store, bought a bright yellow smiley card, and put it on the nightstand. I bought new comfy sheets, rearranged the bedroom to create a sense of belonging, and added some living plants by the windows. Now my new wake-up routine included hearing soft music, looking at the bright card to remind myself of my desire, seeing the life from my plants surrounding me, and inviting the cat to lie with me on my fresh sheets.

Those new choices seemed to be taking me in the right direction, but I did not yet detect any considerable difference in my initial wake-up anxiety. Despite all of my actions, success remained elusive. Nevertheless, giving up was not an option. Not knowing where else to turn, I once again allowed inspiration to guide my actions. Whenever I would feel lost or stuck, it seemed inspiration was able to offer yet another creative possible solution.

I now wondered if a more pampering bathroom routine would help. New plush towels and soft bathroom rugs offered a warmer surrounding. Instead of immediately turning on harsh lights, I installed a dimmer switch. I bought a decorative candle that I lit every morning just for me. I felt special lighting the candle each morning. I placed a deck of inspirational sayings on my bathroom sink counter. This allowed me to acknowledge my initial mood, but then contemplate a different mood from one of the cards while in the shower.

Yet, I failed to find success. What else could I do? I had an epiphany—I had not yet addressed my nighttime ritual. I decided to write in the journal *before* going to bed. Each night, I wrote down my blessings and listed five positive aspects of my day. I also wrote a list of five things about myself that made me proud. I described my intention to feel wonderful, alive, and filled with comfort in the morning. I fell asleep focused on the positive aspects of my day and my intention for how I wanted to feel when I woke up.

One day, I woke up without the feeling of dread. I was not sure exactly when it had happened or how long it took, but I simply realized one morning that my sense of uneasiness was absent. I recognized that I felt considerably more comfortable. Which step was the one that actually worked? In truth, each failed, yet the combination was ultimately successful. Each was a piece of the puzzle, and each step led to the next step. The creative actions were cumulative. In each step, inspiration combined with the committed action of logic to create an ultimate success!

In this example, you can see that the inspired steps by themselves do not seem overly significant. Will a bright yellow smiley card make you feel better? In isolation, it will not. Will buying a dimmer switch change the mood of your day? No. However, when you invite your creativity to play a role in the manifestation of your goal, you will hear or sense numerous possibilities for action. Each step may seem small or insignificant, and, in isolation, they are. However, in the course of achieving your objective, each is meaningful. What matters is that you choose a direction to travel towards, invite your creative spirit to play a role in developing your solutions, and take action to make your dreams real.

The story above is a typical representation of how goals evolve into eventual success. As you move forward on your eating or weight journey, it might be helpful to reflect on the principles outlined above:

1. Identify your desired outcome, and direct your energy toward the creation of that desire.

2. Acknowledge and face your feelings and emotions. Running away from them will not make them disappear.

3. Identify your underlying motivations for wanting what you want. What do you want to feel? What self-supporting beliefs do you want to generate? These reasons ultimately fuel an intense desire for success, even when success is elusive.

4. There is great power in writing down your goals and intentions.

5. Set doable, positive, creative goals. Many of these inspired actions seem to have little or nothing to do with eating, food, or weight but will nonetheless have a significant impact on your ability to move beyond overeating.

6. Find and create happiness along the way, rather than having the unrealistic expectation that ceasing to overeat or losing weight will result in happiness.

7. Get personally involved in your goal. Instead of blindly following a diet or plan provided by someone else, interject your knowledge. Evaluate your actions, modify your approach based on your experiences, and allow yourself to be creative in your approach.

8. Take action on a daily basis.

9. Allow your actions to be cumulative. Just because something does not seem to provide the entire answer, notice if your action is contributing to a better life. If so, keep it in place while you add another action into your mix.

10. Deal with setbacks and failures in a constructive way.

11. Do not give up even when nothing seems to be working.

By setting a goal and taking action, you begin the process of developing a belief in your impending success. Taking steps everyday allows you to take a stand for what you want, place your energy into something that is important to you, and take control of how you feel. Success does not tend to happen overnight but rather by a series of cumulative actions. Motivational expert Zig Ziglar said it well when he stated, "The basic goal-reaching principle is to understand that you go as far as you can see, and when you get there, you will always be able to see farther." By continuing to take action until you succeed, you cultivate a new attitude of, "Yes, I can."

The #1 Secret to Making Your Goal Happen— Take Inspired Action Every Day!

Take action every day. This sounds like simple advice, but it could be the most powerful wisdom provided in this entire book. Choose a direction and *take action every single day*.

Whatever you want, it is not real until you make it real. Without getting your idea out of your mind and into a tangible form, it is just a possibility. When you take physical action, you immediately move beyond persuading yourself that you can have what you want. You say "yes" to your desires through your actions. No matter how small your action, you begin to turn your wish into reality. Maybe you do not know exactly how to get from where you are today to where you want to be in the future. It does not matter. Be aware of your larger goal, and then take daily, confident action, even if it is a small action, in the direction of your desired goal. Be willing to channel your energy into putting one foot in front of the other. Every step is important as you continuously act to improve your life.

Leonardo da Vinci, a genius continually driven to elevate humanity stated, "I have been impressed with the urgency of doing. Knowing is not enough; we must apply. Being willing is not enough; we must do." Day in and day out, do something to further yourself on your journey. Even just one action *every day*—not every other day or every third day—means you have chosen to align yourself with your desires. Life often seems to get in the way, but despite busy work schedules or at-home crises, only you can make a daily, proactive choice to bring the change you want into your reality.

Taking any type of action is important. Yet, you already know that sometimes we base our actions on things we think we "should" be doing. Those actions tend to kill motivation. Check with your heart and find the action that feels inspired. Invite the actions that support your dreams and expand the kind of emotions you want to be feeling. When your action comes from your heart, the effort is not as difficult. Rather than chasing after your goal, look into your heart to find the right action for right now. Allow your choices and actions to be creative, adaptable, and filled with possibility:

Be creative—Typically, problem solving involves thinking about what has worked in the past. We consider the same solutions repeatedly. Creative ideas are outside of the box. They are possible solutions and new ideas that have the potential to lead to desired results. To invoke your creative thinking and creative actions, you do not have to be a special type of person—everyone can do it. Creativity is a skill and talent that can be developed through practice. To get your creative solutions flowing, invoke these elements:

- **See problems as interesting and acceptable**. We often see problems or challenges in life as unacceptable. We avoid pain or suppress it, and in doing so do not listen to the symptoms that are there to tell us something important.

Creative people accept problems as a natural and normal part of life. They understand that moving through these challenges will allow them to reach greater heights of skill, ability, or talent.

- **Become curious**. Curiosity allows you to shed new light on your personal challenges. Look at your problem from multiple angles and learn to ask "why" and "what if" and "I wonder . . ." questions to awaken your creativity. Your questions are a way to explore, examine, and play with things from new angles and perspectives. Take out your journal and begin to look at your situation with curiosity. Become an explorer! When do you eat? How does that help you? What would happen if you did not suppress your emotion? Curiosity allows you to generate alternative ways of responding to your situation.

- **Confront challenge**. When facing a difficult situation, most of us would rather retreat and avoid uncomfortable anxiety and fear. In truth, backing away from your challenge does relieve the anxiety, at least temporarily. In the long-term, avoiding action can lead to lowered self-esteem, feeling powerless and frustrated, and sabotaging your success. Find new ways to face your challenge rather than running from it. Begin to ask yourself, "How can I overcome this?"

- **Constructively Complain:** Articulate what is wrong with your world, and allow your discontent to be a motivation to do something.

Develop optimism—When things go wrong in life some people rise to the occasion with expectant spirits while others respond with self-doubt and hopelessness. The first group is optimistic and can generally withstand their challenges without falling apart. They will keep trying new solutions until they succeed. The second group has a tendency to descend into a spiral of gloom and doom when facing a challenge. The optimists are in the habit of thinking, "I can handle this," when things go wrong. The "doom and gloomers" tend to think, "This is more than I can tolerate." When things go wrong, pessimists tend to have hopeless thoughts. They tell themselves:

—This is too much.

—It is overwhelming.

—This is out of control.

—I will never get it right.

—I cannot stand it.

—I cannot bear this.

Many people struggling to overcome eating issues view their challenges and setbacks as evidence that they will never succeed. They create overly intense states, feeling their experience is too much to handle, too overwhelming, or out of control. They may also criticize themselves for having to face this challenge, attacking themselves with hate, judgment, and blame. The challenge is viewed as an internal weakness that is inescapable. If they overeat they tend to say, "Since I've already screwed up, all is lost. I'm a loser. It's hopeless, so I might as well indulge myself." The setback is more proof that they can never have what they want. Additionally, the setback overshadows, or even seemingly undoes, any forward movement they have had.

When you allow yourself to become more optimistic, you also open yourself to new possibilities. You look to a more positive future and begin to wonder how you can move through this problem. Empower yourself to become your own best cheerleader. Learn how to speak to yourself more kindly, the way a loving friend might. You might consider saying, "Things didn't go well today, but there's a lot to be learned from this experience. I forgive and love myself even though this happened. I can get through this situation and be stronger than I was before." With an optimistic attitude, you free yourself to look within for creative solutions.

Be adaptable——Inside, you will always know which action is most right for you. You will sense which action you *think you should* be taking. Yet, if you look closely, there is also a sense of another type of action that would leave you feeling lighter and proud of yourself. You get to choose if you will motivate yourself because of guilt and heaviness, or if you will move forward with the action that you know is the appropriate action for you right now. Be flexible when choosing your actions. Look at things from multiple points of view and choose the actions that will bring higher levels of energy, motivation, pride, or movement.

See Possibilities—Have you heard the expression about not being able to see the forest for the trees? This expression is used when a person is focusing too much on a specific problem and missing the point. They become overly concerned with detail and fail to see the whole situation. Step back often from the thick of things and see your big picture. Allow your actions to connect the essence of your dreams to reality. What is the larger fundamental nature of your goal? How does what you are doing and how you are doing it fit into the big picture?

As long as you continue your course of daily-inspired action, you are moving forward. Begin every day with the question, "What can I do today to take action?" Look at your situation with curiosity and optimism, and allow yourself to discover an action that feels right for today. Check within and assess whether that action is something you can and will follow through. Actions that are not completed rob you of energy and motivation.

Use the following accountability worksheet: *Did I Take At Least One Action Today?* as an easy way to track your actions. Simply write down the month and begin on today's date. At the end of the day, simply check the "Yes" or "No" column of whether you took action or choose not to take action. This moves you away from the motivation-diluting "I'll try" toward a take-action scenario. You plainly acknowledge to yourself whether or not you took action. Then briefly write down your action. The act of recording your action provides instantaneous feedback and strengthens feelings of forward-movement, possibility, and pride.

Accountability Worksheet

Did I Take At Least One Action Today?

Month _____   Year _____

Date	Yes?	No?	Action
1	____	____	_____
2	____	____	_____
3	____	____	_____
4	____	____	_____
5	____	____	_____
6	____	____	_____
7	____	____	_____
8	____	____	_____
9	____	____	_____
10	____	____	_____
11	____	____	_____
12	____	____	_____
13	____	____	_____
14	____	____	_____
15	____	____	_____
16	____	____	_____
17	____	____	_____
18	____	____	_____
19	____	____	_____
20	____	____	_____
21	____	____	_____
22	____	____	_____

23 ____ ____ _____

24 ____ ____ _____

25 ____ ____ _____

26 ____ ____ _____

27 ____ ____ _____

28 ____ ____ _____

29 ____ ____ _____

30 ____ ____ _____

31 ____ ____ _____

Is Your Goal in Balance?

While most everyday decisions do not require action plans, your goal is different. For instance, you do not need to develop a series of balanced steps to figure out how to get your closet organized. You just make a decision, dig in, and begin arranging. Your eating or weight goal is different because it is a big goal. It is not just about eating differently; it is about clearing out foundational beliefs, changing perceptions, and creating a new way of living. That is a complex process, not a single event. During this process you are learning to create balance in your life as you allocate your time differently, make your needs a priority, develop a positive support system, and alter old conditioning that held you back. To achieve your goal requires different types of actions that span across many diverse areas of your life. Some actions reduce stress levels, others increase your ability to play more, while yet others serve to increase your confidence.

As you already know, ending overeating, emotional eating, or compulsive types of eating behaviors involves more than an "eat less, exercise more" approach. You need an action plan that includes the acquisition of new life skills. These actions allow you to take responsibility for your life, learn ways of handling your self, and become the person you want to become. What actions will you take to take care of your internal world— your fears, your limiting beliefs, your anxiety, and your feelings and emotions? Review the list below and highlight the areas of your life that require attention and planned action to achieve your goal:

- Develop a self-supportive attitude
- Reconnect with the feeling of being happy and healthy
- Build greater confidence
- Maintain self-responsibility
- Set boundaries
- Increase positive motivation
- Raise self-esteem
- Learn to relax
- Amplify self-love and self-caring
- Listen to intuition and inner guidance
- Decrease worry and anxiety
- Get organized and remove clutter from your life
- Eat with pleasure
- Gain body trust
- Increase play and relaxation
- Learn to express emotions

Understanding that your actions and efforts will span many areas of your life helps you see beyond the immediate problem of eating and weight loss. Your focus shifts to the solution of developing a happier life by placing yourself as a priority and taking care of all your needs. Balanced actions help you replenish your personal motivation and grow as a person. Using the list above and the form below, creatively brainstorm for new actions that will help bring greater balance into your life. See the following page for an example to inspire you:

Balanced Goal Worksheet Example

Increase Positive Motivation Energy	**Stress and Relaxation Strategies**
• Fill out *all* the forms in this guide • Attend a personal development workshop • Associate with positive people • Read inspiring books • Begin a journal • Visualize a successful completion of the goal	• Buy meditation tapes and listen • Create a daily priority list • Listen to classical music on drive home • Breathe to let go of tension • Enroll in yoga class • Do not rely on memory, write things down • Take vacation time every 3 months
Increase Enjoyment of Food	**Increase Joy of Life**
• Take a cooking class • Buy a set of beautiful dishes • Inhale food aroma before eating • 2x/week, prepare meal for self & enjoy • Eat at dinner table with plates and silverware • Entertain: Have small dinner party	• Watch movies that make me laugh • Go to sleep on time • Sleep only the amount of time needed • Spend time with enjoyable people • Clean out clutter and organize • Plan a fun evening and enjoy it • Buy clothes that fit and feel good • Work regular hours • Throw out outdated books and clothes • Create a personal space at home
Get in Touch with My Body and Senses	
• Have weekly 20 min. chair massage • Take 10 min. walk every morning • Buy myself flowers & place in kitchen • Paint my personal space a bright color • Give and receive more hugs • Enroll in a pottery class	**Increase Self-Acceptance**
	• Talk supportively to my body daily • Participate in enjoyable activities • Allow upbeat and positive self-talk • Nightly, list 5 positive self qualities
Confidence Skills to Learn	**Support System**
• Journal weekly to explore emotions • Complete 1 small task successfully today • Make 2 daily conscious decisions, follow through, and recognize success • Learn to say "no!" • Allow failure . . . it's part of the journey • Use praise for effort to build confidence • Visualize success	• List names & numbers of friends to call
	Other
	• •

Balanced Goal Worksheet

Increase Positive Motivation Energy:

_____

_____

_____

_____

_____

Stress and Relaxation Strategies:

_____

_____

_____

_____

_____

Increase Enjoyment of Food:

_____

_____

_____

_____

_____

Increase Joy of Life:

_____

_____

_____

_____

_____

Get in Touch with My Body and Senses:

_____

_____

_____

_____

Increase Self-Acceptance:

_____

_____

_____

_____

Confidence Skills to Learn: Names & Numbers of Support People:

_____   _____

_____   _____

_____   _____

_____   _____

_____   _____

Focus on Success

This particular goal of yours—the goal of eating differently or transforming your body—is an extremely complex goal. Even though many promises of "easy" weight loss abound, there is no simple way to success. This is because you are not solving the problem of eating or weighing less. If that were all you were doing, you could plug in any diet plan, exercise more, and be on your way in no time. That is not the case here. You are engaged in the process of a transformation of your very core beliefs. This specific goal is one that will help you become clearer about your own identity, integrate new skills and coping strategies into your routine, and enter a new stage of your life.

Your journey involves moving away from relying on external sources of feeling good and moving into the discovery of self-love. You have chosen to move away from the comfort offered by food and, in its place, enlarge the sweetness and fullness of your life from the inside. You will ask meaningful questions of yourself, expand your thinking beyond your current limitations, and achieve new potentials for your life.

You set a goal to revisit your central beliefs and attitudes in order to create a new sense of possibility. This requires stepping out of your comfort zone and making decisions that you are not used to making. During this journey, you will find yourself frantically trying to apply familiar solutions to the problem, but they just do not work anymore. This often leads to confusion, despair, and a sense of helplessness as you experience a sense of being stuck without options. To move beyond this point entails entering into an exploration of emotions, love, and body acceptance in ways never previously considered. You might have thought you were "trying to win the war over weight," but in truth, your journey is an adventure to uncover hidden creativity, develop a deeper love of self, heal old wounds, release resentments, and promote serenity.

Despite the upheaval that will occur with this reconstruction of your beliefs, this process will bring you countless opportunities to recognize inner strength and increase happiness. The goal you chose, and its accompanying challenges, includes your most important heart-felt wish for yourself—to give yourself the love, worthiness, safety, and success you have always wanted. In the end, you are deciding if you are willing to trade persistent work and effort to gain a happier life. This may well be the most difficult undertaking you will ever face. Metaphorically, it is as if you are lifting yourself out of quicksand. You are choosing to be accountable for being in the quicksand to begin with and accepting responsibility for doing the difficult work of getting out. It may not be fair that this is your task, and others may have contributed to your predicament. Nonetheless, here you are. It is your choice to either remain here in the quicksand or do whatever is necessary to get out.

The illusion imperative to dismiss is that your happier life will arrive at the end of the goal. Instead, it comes with each effort you put forth. Happiness grows as you realize that each action you take to lift yourself a little further out of the quicksand is because you want to live differently. You feel joy as you comprehend that you do love yourself; you do not want to live your life forever in the quicksand. Because of that realization, you now want to enlarge your life and to reshape your identity.

The motivation to change requires intrinsic ongoing motivation. This type of motivation is your inner desire to achieve something meaningful to you. Like the old adage about being able to lead a horse to water but not being able to make him drink, nothing and no one can motivate you to do something. Others can provide an occasional boost to your inspiration, but ultimately long-term, persistent motivation comes from within you.

Fear, intimidation, or self-critical thoughts are one type of motivator. However, these kinds of motivators usually only prompt action for the short-term. Long-term motivation takes place when you see the value of your goal and you feel good because of that observation. Yet, how can you feel good when you do not yet have your outcome? Recognize that your goal originated in your heart and in your spirit. Your love of self prompted you to want to have a different or more delightful human experience. The "you" who is having this current experience is the same "you" who will be enjoying or living the next experience. You can feel good now because you see the bigger scheme of things. Even though you do not have your outcome, you can make your journey a heart-centered enterprise.

This ability to exude positivity into your journey is not going to happen on its own. Every step of your goal, whether successful or unsuccessful, requires feedback and encouragement. Every task is an opportunity to nurture the qualities you seek. It is imperative that you prepare in advance a system to salute each effort and accomplishment. Train yourself to be as vigilant in looking for examples of self-loving behavior as you are in noticing your transgressions.

Get into the habit of acknowledging your efforts, actions, and achievements. Provide recognition in some sort of tangible way. This means writing your efforts and successes down and rewarding them in a real way. By recognizing your efforts, you move beyond being "good" or "bad" and instead learn how to take responsibility for your life. You are not a bad person when you binge or eat certain foods. You are just engaging in one type of activity to make "you" feel better. When you write down your efforts, you notice that certain decisions move you closer to your desire to feel better in new and different ways, while other choices move you further away. As you affirm each effort, you will consciously begin to realize that success, confidence, and happiness are choices. You have free will to live your life in the manner you choose.

The object of acknowledging your efforts and successes is not in "earning" a reward. Rather, it is in becoming aware that your choices affect the quality of your own life. Keep in mind that your praise, love, and affection are not rewards for being a "good" person. Your purpose is not becoming a better, more socially acceptable person, but revealing yourself as a person who is loving of self, capable of joy, and worthy of achieving a more desirable life experience.

Along each and every step of the way, accept responsibility for changing and take credit for your hard work. Delight in your efforts and accomplishments. Every day, take a few minutes to list all your attempts at improvement. Do not merely highlight the successes but stress each endeavor. No matter how minute, each undertaking deserves recognition. Place a checkmark on your calendar, get a hug from your partner, or put some money in a jar for each effort and for each success. Be creative and allow your acknowledgment to be tangible, immediate, and personally meaningful.

Make time to reflect on effort expended and success achieved. Continue providing recognition and encouragement. Do not leave this important part of your journey to chance. Take the time right now to design your own list of rewards and recognitions. You can always modify them in the future. However, right now, put down on paper a list of potential incentives for reaching important benchmarks.

Note that different people can have quite different motivators. For example, some people are motivated by money, others by clothes, and others by social interaction. However, you can use the following lists to stimulate your own creative thinking:

Effort Acknowledgment

The easiest way to assail your enthusiasm or confidence is to overlook your effort. Effort does not mean that you achieved success. It means that you put forth honest, deliberate energy and action toward your goal. Effort includes the many self-supportive actions that lead to greater happiness. Effort includes pre-planning your success strategy, visualizing success, encouraging self-talk, taking a bath to relieve stress, or consciously taking a breath and finding center instead of reacting from autopilot. Effort also includes, for example, devising and implementing a plan to avoid a binge after work, even if that plan did not ultimately succeed. Effort includes each attempt you decide to say "no" to your desire to eat and "yes" to another alternative action. Even if your alternate action failed and you then resorted once again to using food to feel better, you still applied effort. That effort needs your encouragement and recognition.

Internally, you are starving for reassurance, acceptance, or validation. The recognition you most seek is not from other people but, instead, from within yourself. Giving yourself positive feedback is an expression of gratitude that builds self-confidence and perseverance. Every ounce of effort deserves a sincere "thank you." For example, working your way through this book has entailed effort. How will you acknowledge that you not only took the time to read this guide but that you also engaged effort in completing the exercises? Develop a habit of listing your efforts and providing relevant or inspiring recognition of your contributions. Decide in advance that you will recognize your efforts on a daily basis by writing them down. In addition, you may also decide that, for example, with every ten efforts put forth you will give yourself one reward from your list. The following are some possible "thank you" ideas to keep yourself encouraged, feeling good, and revitalized to take the next step:

- Place a bird feeder outside your office window.

- Take thirty minutes and sit in a quiet park.

- Wear an expressive button to advertise your efforts to the world.

- Go grocery shopping and contribute the food to your local food bank.

- Visit your local no-kill animal shelter and donate ten dollars.

- Browse through a local card shop and stock up on thoughtful notes.

- Start an herb garden in your kitchen window.

- Take yourself on a date.

- Organize a drawer or a shelf that has been bugging you.

- Listen to a special and specific inspirational song to celebrate your efforts.

- Place a small group of celebration balloons in your office or kitchen to boost your morale.

- Share a hug of success with your friends, family, or partner.

Success Acknowledgment

Achieving goals is about building new actions and habits. Rather than criticizing unwanted behaviors, rewarding each successful accomplishment develops a stronger connection to what you want. Adults, just like children, continue or repeat behaviors that are recognized, praised, and rewarded. Even something as simple as "Good job!" or a silver star placed on your calendar can pump up your level of confidence.

Confidence is an internal judgment of how sure you are of your ability to succeed in your goal. People often lack confidence because they do not acknowledge achievement. If you never celebrate your many successes—both small and large—then you will start resenting all the work involved in attaining your desire. If you do not take the time to congratulate yourself, who will? Sometimes, people dismiss or demean what they have done. They may ignore the achievement as if it never happened or minimize their success by saying something like, "It was not all that good."

Another confidence killer is seeing the goal as one large all-or-nothing entity. In this approach, success or failure is determined by the outcome. Using this strategy, even if you did succeed, how long would you have to wait before acknowledging your ultimate success? One month? One year? What if you revert back to your old eating habits one time, six months down the road? Have you failed overall? Notice how unfair, demotivating, and defeating that course of action can be.

Increase your confidence by recognizing each success. Define, in advance, what your definition of a success is, and create a list of tangible rewards designed to celebrate those benchmarks. For example, for every fifth time you choose to calm yourself by going for a walk outside instead of eating, you will give yourself a specified recognition or reward. Here are some ideas to get you started in your efforts to say, "Wow! Look what I did!"

- Detail your car or have someone else do it for you.

- Hugs and back-pats: Never underestimate the importance of being touched by someone.

- Get a twenty-minute chair massage.

- Discover a local museum or tourist site that you have never visited.

- Plant a small tree in your backyard.

- Go to the library and check out a new motivational book or CD.

- Write a poem about your accomplishments and post it on your refrigerator.

- Hire a house-cleaning service to whip your home into shape.

- Rearrange your closet and organize your drawers. When you clear space, you also allow energy to flow in new ways.

- Order some flowers to be delivered to you.

- Write and mail yourself a congratulatory card.

- Write in your journal about your success and share it with a friend.

Milestone Acknowledgment

The path toward ultimate success will be a long one. Along the way, you will encounter significant milestones. These points of reference are passed after facing a fear, overcoming a challenge, or stepping beyond a major obstacle. For each milestone reached, give yourself a big round of applause! This achievement deserves a promotion, a raise, and a celebration. Do not hold back! Let your imagination run wild in planning what goodies await you after these monumental accomplishments!

- Go back to the shelter and take home of one of those adorable dogs or cats.

- Throw a potluck party and invite your friends to celebrate your success with you.

- Go to a trophy shop and have one personally engraved with your success.

- Create a Success Certificate for yourself, frame it, and place it proudly in your office or home.

- Get a small tattoo and permanently celebrate your accomplishment.

- Receive a new ear piercing and publicly declare your joy in succeeding.

- Buy yourself a real diamond stud to place in that new ear piercing.

- Name a star after yourself.

- Send yourself a big bouquet of flowers for your special milestone.

- Give yourself a day off from work or a day off from your house cleaning chores.

Focus on Success Worksheet

Date: _____   Mon   Tues   Wed   Thur   Fri   Sat   Sun

Overall Goal: _____

_____

_____

List of Effort Recognitions	List of Success Recognitions	List of Milestone Recognitions
1.	1.	1.
2.	2.	2.
3.	3.	3.
4.	4.	4.
5.	5.	5.
6.	6.	6.
7.	7.	7.
8.	8.	8.

My reinforcement **today** for putting *effort* into my goal: _____

_____

Every (define # of days) _____ day of achieving the *success* of (define the success)

_____ my acknowledgment is:

_____

Observance of this specific *milestone* (define milestone)_____ is:

_____

Celebration at the *completion* of my goal:

_____

The Power of Personal Responsibility

In the beginning, it is easy to feel excitement about your goal-achieving venture. It is shiny-new and filled with the sparkle of new potential. But sooner or later, something is likely to change your rosy outlook. Perhaps on second glance the task will seem too daunting. You may realize the process is more involved, complicated, or time-consuming than you imagined. You are going to procrastinate, become distracted, and grow weary or bored. As soon as you reach a point in your evolution that requires more self-discipline or strength of will than you believe you possess, you will be tempted to quit. One day, you may find yourself asking if your goal is worth the hassle.

In truth, your goal is not going to be easy to obtain. No goal ever is. Most likely, you will want to abandon your goals and go back to eating when things are tough. When this happens, we want to cast blame on people and situations for our predicament. For example, it is not fair that your struggle involves food. You deserve to eat what you want without any consequences. In the past you soothed yourself with food when obstacles arose, now how are you to provide yourself with comfort or distraction? Forget waiting for some illusionary goal, the food is immediate and tangible. You will want to run away from the big picture of your life and choose the cookie, cake, or burger and fries instead. You will want to trade your hope of creating a better future for a fleeting tidbit of feeling good right now. After all, it is not your fault that you are in this situation.

In truth, there are many contributing factors to why you are dealing with food and weight. Your parents set the stage for your overeating. Your siblings, religion, and teachers all helped mold a negative view of how the world works. Your genes are to blame for your sluggish metabolism. Fast food restaurants are responsible for your growing waistline with their high-fat-content foods and super-sized meals. Your boss is responsible because of all the stress he or she creates. The list of causative factors is long. Personal responsibility is the ability to accept that whether or not you are responsible, you decide to act as though you are because it gives you the power to choose differently.

Most everyone, possibly even you, wants the easy path. You want what you want, when you want it, without having to work so hard for it. You do not want to struggle. You do not want to do unpleasant or difficult things. You really do not want to step out of your comfort zone. You do not want to risk failure or, sometimes, even success. You want to apply the minimum amount of effort in order to get your desired outcome. However, that is not the purpose of your adventure. Despite everything, you have grown tired of the way you live now. Maybe you have even grown bored of dealing with your food or weight issues. You *really* do want to pull yourself out of your problems into a new life.

Personal responsibility is what lifts you out of the murky stagnancy of your life. Your choice to take action, even when faced with an almost overwhelming desire not to, releases inner power. If you take action, you reclaim your life. If you do not take action, you continue to believe you are a victim. Your responsibility includes facing the moments when you want to quit—when you think things are impossible—and making a new decision. No one else is in charge of changing your eating patterns. No one else is supposed to be accountable for your actions. It is your responsibility alone to declare what you want and exert the effort to pursue it.

What does is mean to be responsible for your self? It means developing enthusiasm for life and learning to focus your thoughts and actions in a direction that is meaningful. Raising your level of desire and taking action to pursue goals is no simple task, but it is one all human beings face as we evolve to higher levels of authenticity and aliveness. The list below serves as a reminder that it is within our own power to create new habits that support our ever-expanding joy, love, health, and life.

- I alone have the responsibility to bring pleasure and satisfaction to my life.

- I have the responsibility to bless myself with unconditional love and acceptance.

- I have the responsibility to build myself up and motivate myself with positive self-talk.

- I have the responsibility to choose the direction of my life.

- I have the responsibility to make decisions and follow through with them.

- I have the responsibility to build beliefs that create my success.

- I have the responsibility to recognize I am the cause of my choices.

- I have the responsibility to view failures and effort as necessary steps along the path to success.

- I have the responsibility to experience inner peace.

- I have the responsibility to persist until I succeed.

Personal responsibility is filled with love and is your key to freedom. You have the ability to turn your life around and reclaim your power. However, the only way to retrieve your power is to face inner resistance and move forward anyway. Doing this is difficult beyond description. It will feel impossible, unfair, and emotional. Yet, once you move beyond your inertia and accept personal responsibility for the outcome of your life, you will taste the delicious freedom of your own power. Personal responsibility involves asking yourself: Will you support you in your desire to live differently, even when times get tough? Will you do what it takes to give yourself what you most want?

Taking new action is easier said than done because you are in the process of deciding whether it would be in your best interests to take control of your life in a new way. You are deciding to look beneath the patterns of eating and embrace the pain you have been suppressing. That is not something easily accomplished. You have to give up the story of who hurt you or who holds the blame for your problems. You have to fill the gap between your current state and your future desired state. Some things need to change, while others need to be reinforced. The issue you face is whether you decide that you deserve more from life or whether you continue to accept the status quo. Is it your place to *give yourself* more than you have right now?

What will you do when you reach an obstacle in your pathway? What will you do when things do not go right or you do not think you can move forward? If you stop, you preserve the belief that you do not possess the ability to have what you want. However, if you can accept responsibility that where you are right now is difficult and seems impossible but take action anyway despite resistance, you will find you are no longer powerless or stuck. You can decide to move forward even when the situation seems thicker than molasses. You begin to recognize yourself as a capable creator, and that you are indeed fully capable of taking action no matter what the circumstances appear to be.

Every time you step beyond fear, procrastination, doubt, confusion, or worry you gain deeper insight into who you are and what you are capable of achieving. Every challenge, setback, or failure is necessary to uncover the strength that allows you to choose a life that is constructive rather than destructive. Every difficult emotion gives you the opportunity to decide that your goal was important when you started and that your goal remains important. You will remember your compelling reason and fall in love with your goal all over again. Despite resistance, you look inside for inspiration and take action.

Personal responsibility shows you, in a way that is unavoidable, that you are in charge of creating the life you are living. No matter what has happened, what tragedies have befallen you, or what you believe about yourself, you are always involved in the process of creating your own life. Everything you are, in this moment, stems from what you have believed and the choices you have made. Yesterday's beliefs, behaviors, and actions established today's results. The choices you make at this juncture create the life you will lead tomorrow.

Personal responsibility includes the following:

- Acknowledging that you determine who you are and how your life evolves.

- Choosing a specific goal or direction that is important to you.

- Making sure your goal is meaningful to your heart and spirit.

- Moving your goal and needs to the top of your priority list.

- Taking daily action that allows you feel the way you want to feel.

- Acting with love and compassion for yourself.

- Becoming your own best cheerleader—it is your job to support and validate your efforts.

- Accepting that your goal will take you out of your comfort zone.

- Acknowledging excuses as excuses and discovering creative ways to move beyond them.

- Accepting that blaming others or yourself does not move you forward to your desired outcome.

- Determining how your self-esteem will develop.

- Taking an honest inventory of your strengths, abilities, talents, and positive characteristics.

- Deciding that your burden may be unfair, but it is up to you to give your experiences value, meaning, and direction.

Personal responsibility matures when you provide yourself with regular feedback. Take a few minutes now and create a list of your personal responsibilities as it relates to moving forward with your goal. When you reach a challenge, are you someone who takes personal responsibility for your actions?

My Personal Responsibilities Include:

1. _____

2. _____

3. _____

4. _____

5. _____

6. _____

7. _____

8. _____

9. _____

10. _____

Face Your Excuses and End Them

Imagine for a moment that you and your best friend arrange to meet for dinner and the symphony this evening. Your friend agrees to pick you up at your house at six. In anticipation, you plan your day around the event making sure all your work tasks and home chores are finished so you can enjoy the evening. You set aside time to bathe, get dressed, and look attractive. Six o'clock arrives, yet your friend does not. After about fifteen minutes, you call to see what the delay is. She answers the phone and gasps that she is so very sorry. She claims something important came up, and she completely forgot about your evening plans.

Even though you are an understanding person, this event was important to you. If this is the first time your friend broke her date with you, chances are you will get over your feelings, give her the benefit of doubt, and chalk up her actions to a real unavoidable situation. However, what if your friend does the same thing to you again next week? What if you discover that she has a pattern of saying one thing but doing another? Most likely, you will feel betrayed. Whether she said so directly or not, her actions state that she has priorities that are more important than keeping her word to you. Her forgetfulness and excuses are an indicator that she does not place much importance on the agreements she makes with you. When she breaks her promises, your relationship with her begins to fill with anger, resentment, and a loss of trust.

Now, imagine that your friend continues this pattern of making excuses and breaking her promises to you. Only, because you are afraid of conflict and you are anxious about standing up for your own needs, you do not confront the situation. Instead of learning from the experience and taking an assertive new course, you continue making plans and being disappointed time and time again. Every time your friend fails to follow through with her word, you believe you are a victim. Inside you become hard and bitter, not trusting her, yet still making plans. Instead of talking to her, taking self-responsible action, and setting personal boundaries, you naively withhold and withdraw. Your relationship lacks respect and becomes unsafe and untrustworthy. You eventually become angry and bitter. As the relationship becomes more negative, you feel increasingly unloved and dishonored.

When you set your goal, you commit to love and cherish it. You agree to show up and take action. There is an unspoken agreement to be devoted to nurturing the developing relationship between you and your desire. However, many of us make promises and commitments to ourselves that we fully intend to keep—if nothing else gets in the way, or if the task does not involve discomfort. Then we make up excuses of why we cannot take action. These excuses are the lies we tell to ourselves and that we believe to be true. However, if we are willing to take a closer look at our excuses, we will see that there is always a creative solution to any obstacle.

Being faithful to the process involves being honest, open, and real. Challenges, obstacles, and excuses are expected and unavoidable. Your choices will involve discomfort. The important point is, what will you do when your excuses appear? Will you respect yourself and honestly work through the conflict? Will you make the effort to look at what went wrong and modify your course of future action? Alternatively, will you give yourself an excuse and then pretend that everything is fine? Will you buy into your own excuse without confronting yourself?

When you set your goal, it is a decision made from your core to work toward something that is important to your heart and to your life. Your excuses are sort of like your friend in the story above. Some part of you has an objection or a different agenda. When you hear this excuse and do not follow through, then avoid confronting the excuse, you create distance rather than intimacy in the relationship between you and your goal. You tell yourself through action that you and your needs are unimportant. The Shakespearean character Polonius said, *"To thine own self be true."* Every time you buy into your own excuse, you betray yourself. You agree to show up and then do not. Then, you pretend your actions are acceptable. No wonder you feel resentful, bitter, and unfulfilled. You are an untrustworthy partner—unreliable, dishonest, and disrespectful. It is easy to see why we rely so heavily on pleasing others. We become dependent on other people for our well-being rather than asserting ourselves in our own lives.

Excuses can be sophisticated and quite legitimate. No matter how realistic the excuse seems, ultimately we are only fooling ourselves. Excuses lay the blame for failure on external causes rather than our own lack of determination or skill ability. We find believable reasons for our behavior as opposed to seeking out the real explanation.

Some of the most common excuses include the following:

- *Denial of responsibility*: blaming failure on circumstances and feeling a victim of influences beyond your control.

- *Projection of blame*: blaming failure on other people.

- *Procrastination*: not placing your needs and goals as a top priority; putting off until tomorrow what you can accomplish today.

- *Justifying*: explaining the reason for things.

- *Creative avoidance or self-deceit*: dodging responsibility by getting busy, taking care of other people, or being distracted by anything that comes along.

Nothing will kill motivation and morale faster than ignoring the problems, challenges, and excuses that arise. To succeed in creating a better life, learning to identify excuses is imperative. Get into the habit of taking your promises seriously. When you know in advance that you have a "no excuses" policy, you choose your actions and commitments more carefully and follow through on them no matter what. To overcome your excuses, learn to recognize how and when you choose to evade action. Then ask yourself to name out loud the denial of responsibility, rationalization, projection, procrastination, or self-deceit excuse used.

The following is a list of some common excuses that seem plausible. In the end, they are simply excuses you give yourself to avoid the work involved in creating a happier life. Every time you buy into your own excuse, you not only continue believing you are a powerless victim, but you also make a choice that says you deserve to feel bad.

- I should be able to . . . , but I cannot.

- I am depressed and do not have the energy.

- Somebody needed my help, and I had to give her all of my attention.

- Something came up, and I had to put my goal on hold.

- I do not feel well today; I am too tired.

- I am not in the mood.

- I am so overweight, I might as well give up.

- I had a lot on my plate.

- Someone died.

- It does not seem important to anyone that I achieve this goal.

- No one wants to help me.

- Someone told me that my goal was not a good idea.

- I am doing all of this work, and I do not see any difference.

- I want someone else to be accountable for my actions.

- Why go on? I see no use in it.

- I will do it Monday.

- I am just lazy.

- Terrible things are always happening to me.

- My parents made me the way I am.

- Self-help books, positive thinking, or the advice of others cannot help me.

My most common excuses include:

1. _____

2. _____

3. _____

4. _____

5. _____

6. _____

7. _____

8. _____

Recognize that excuses are creative justifications for inaction. You are an intelligent being, and as such, you will come up with the most genuine, legitimate-sounding excuses. Ultimately, you are only hurting yourself. You said you wanted to show up for yourself, you became excited, and then at the first sign of trouble, you surrendered. Afterward, you convinced yourself that you had no other choice. This self-deception is not okay; and judgment, blame, anger, contempt, and a sense of helplessness are a few of the consequences of your actions. You deserve self-respect, empowerment, and peace. These inner states are not attained at the end of the goal but each time you provide yourself with honest feedback. A truthful statement such as, "I could have taken that action, but it was difficult and uncomfortable so I choose not to," brings you authority and control over your own life.

How do you get beyond your excuse making? Evaluate your behavior realistically and honestly. Be cognizant of how you are stopping yourself from creating a better life. One quick, yet powerful, tool is to use **rational self-talk**. This simply means identifying your excuse, and then rephrasing it in a more empowering, self-supporting manner. A major problem with making excuses is that they tend to dart into our consciousness, do their damage, and then dart back out again. We barely realize what has happened. Our excuses could be completely wrong and incorrect, but since we do not challenge them, we remain suffering from their harmful effects.

The rational self-talk approach is a simple method to identify excuses and then restructure them into realistic, truthful accounts of the situation or experience. In doing so, you can approach the situation again, only this time with a newly gained freedom of choice. You can choose to take action or choose not to. This creates emotions you can handle and helps you act in ways that promote your goals and happiness.

To benefit from the rational self-talk tool:

1. **Write** down your excuse or the thoughts you experienced when you avoided taking action, and

2. **Identify** a fair, balanced perspective about the situation.

Here are two examples of excuses and rational self-talk:

Excuse: I am not in the mood right now. I am too tired and depressed to take action.

Rational self-talk: I do not have to be in the right mood to take action. I could take action even though I am tired and depressed. It will take effort to get things moving, but once I get started, I will feel better because I did something for myself. Taking this action may not lead to my feeling completely energized and happy, but I will feel somewhat better. Besides, if I wait for the right mood, I may never get started.

Excuse: I have to work and take care of my family first. There is not enough time for me.

Rational self-talk: I do have a busy life, but I realize that I make time for the things and people I find important to me. My goal is important, and if I want to take action, I will need to plan it into my schedule. If I put my needs at the top of my priority list and pick a specific time of day when I take action, I will be able to make progress on my goal, gain energy, and still be able to take care of my family.

Delivered well, feedback can result in positive action and change. Delivered poorly, feedback can result in negativity, hostility, and even rebellion. Use the tools of feedback provided in this guide not as a license to criticize or judge yourself, but to clearly see how excuses lead to a sense of disempowerment and unhappiness. It may be helpful to remember that feedback is information. If you did not take action today, do not be blind to the truth. Write your inactions down in bright red letters. Give yourself an F on your worksheets. The object is not to feel guilt or punishment but to provide an opportunity to notice how avoiding action creates negativity, heaviness, and beliefs of powerlessness. Then you can choose honestly and deliberately whether you wish to continue moving forward.

At this point in your journey, print out twenty-one copies of the following *No More Excuses Worksheets* and set them aside. You can download printable forms at www.AnnetteColby.com/goalforms.

No More Excuses Worksheet

Date: _____   Mon   Tues   Wed   Thur   Fri   Sat   Sun

Issue or Problem: _____

_____

What went wrong? _____

_____

_____

What did I let get in my way? _____

_____

_____

What reasons, explanations, or excuses did I give to let myself off the hook? _____

_____

_____

_____

How do I *feel* about excusing myself from being more fully engaged in my goal? _____

_____

_____

_____

What potential solution can I try? _____

_____

_____

_____

Tying It All Together

Congratulations! Your preparation work is complete. You have successfully laid the foundation to a new life. The *Daily Goal Worksheet* below is a way to bring all the concepts of goal achieving into one simple and organized system. The overall purpose of using these goal sheets is to help you generate greater feelings of empowerment and greater love toward yourself and life. Every step you take, whether in a forward or backward direction, helps you see that you are responsible for increasing your sense of empowerment and joy.

Use these forms to:

- Remind yourself daily of your passionate goal.

- Remain focused on your compelling reason.

- Decide repeatedly that you are worthy of feeling joy.

- Acknowledge how you stop yourself from feeling good.

- Decide if your goal is important enough to you to continue moving forward.

The instructions are simple:

1. Prevailing wisdom tells us: Do something for twenty-one days in a row and it will become a habit. In general, it takes about twenty-one days, or three weeks, to establish a new habit. Toward this end, print out twenty-one *Daily Goal Worksheets*. Collate and assemble them so that the front sheet will be the *Daily Goal Worksheets* and the second sheet will be the *No More Excuses Worksheets*. Divide your worksheets so that you create three stacks of seven forms in each. Staple each stack. Now you have three weeks of forms, pre-printed and divided into small, doable projects.

   You will not be using the forms forever. Instead, they are a powerful tool to help you overcome mental barriers, establish your needs as priorities, become focused on your objectives, and gain momentum. In addition, you will not achieve your goal in three weeks. However, within that time frame you will have learned the essential language of success. If you follow the process, you will understand, and have at your disposal, the tools needed to move forward beyond any internal resistance you may face.

2. Complete the top four items of the *Daily Goal Worksheet* first thing in the morning. Fill in the Date, your Overall Objective, your Compelling Reason, and Today's Action Steps. Choose realistic, doable actions that come from your heart. Choose not what you believe you *should* be doing, but what *feels* right and applicable for today.

3. At the end of the day, complete the rest of the form. Check or cross off the action steps you completed. List your efforts and successes. Use your *No More Excuses Worksheet* to creatively identify potential solutions for today's challenges. Be **positive and self-affirming** when recognizing your efforts and successes. Be **truthful and honest** when acknowledging your excuses.

On the 0 to 100 line, determine in advance what the defining points are. Naturally, zero is the absence of any thought, effort, or action put into your goal for that particular day. However, how do you define 50? How do you define 100? Goals include both effort and action strategies. Effort means that you put forth honest, deliberate energy toward your goal. Effort includes the many self-supportive actions that lead to greater happiness. Some of your efforts include relaxation strategies, breathing and centering, identifying excuses, restructuring your thought processes, and so on. Even if you did not avert a binge or overeating behavior today, does that mean you did not put any effort into your goal? Think carefully about how you define your 0 to 100 line. Utilizing a black-and-white, all or nothing approach can de-motivate and deflate your enthusiasm. Use your 0 to 100 line to encourage accountability, acknowledge effort, and inspire yourself toward ever-increasing happiness and fulfillment.

Daily Goal Worksheet

Date: _____   Mon   Tues   Wed   Thur   Fri   Sat   Sun

Overall Goal or Objective: _____

Compelling Reason: _____

Today's Action Steps:

1. _____

2. _____

3. _____

4. _____

5. _____

Efforts (visualization, intention-setting, affirmations, self-talk, journaling, etc.):

1. _____

2. _____

3. _____

Successes:

1. _____

2. _____

3. _____

Excuses (amusing things I said to myself or did to keep myself from having what I most want):

1. _____

2. _____

3. _____

Challenges, Emotions, & Potential Solutions:

1. _____

2. _____

3. _____

The one area I'm proud of myself today: _____

Effort Put towards goal today (0 = no effort, 100 = maximum effort):

0 _____ 100

I am planning the following event, action, effort, or success to take place tomorrow:

_____

Twenty Tips to Keep You Inspired

Anyone who has set a goal knows how determined and motivated you feel when you first start out. Your goal is clear, you are determined to achieve it, and nothing is going to stop you! Indeed, for the first few weeks, you stick to your plan. You feel that this time your success will be permanent, and you are going to keep going until you reach the end. Somewhere along the way, motivation wanes. Because achieving your goal is dependent on sustained, active participation, it is up to you find new ways to pump up the volume on your motivation levels whenever they begin to drop. Motivation is dependent on two areas: **the belief that you are capable of achieving your goal** and **the desire to do it**. Gear your efforts toward developing these two areas. Success builds on success, so choose your actions wisely.

Below is a list of ideas to increase the two areas of motivation—belief and desire:

1. Imagine your future success and the feelings you will experience when you achieve it.

2. Realize the possibilities—your dream is possible, and you can have what you want.

3. Set a target for the amount of work you will do each day that will lead toward your goal.

4. Be realistic—set daily goals you know you can accomplish.

5. Keep your promises—if you say you are going to do something, do it.

6. Do something every day—just get started no matter how difficult it seems.

7. Build structure into your day—decide exactly when you will take action.

8. Chart your progress—write everything down including every success, effort, failure, challenge, and disappointment.

9. Reward! Reward! Reward!

10. Know why you are striving for goals—review your compelling reason daily.

11. Do not put off joy—do whatever you can to look good and feel good now.

12. Read something inspiring like a biography, quote, or poem.

13. Rediscover your sense of adventure—make your journey more fun!

14. Listen to motivational tapes that encourage you in your actions.

15. Use simple, powerful, motivational words to demonstrate that you value your efforts.

16. Define your own version of success—do not let others define success for you.

17. Focus on your positive efforts and achievements.

18. Give yourself clear, honest feedback without judgment or sugar-coating the facts.

19. Allow yourself to make mistakes and do not punish yourself for them.

20. Recover from failure by picking yourself up . . . begin again!

Chapter Seven

Self-Leadership Skills to Master Your Destiny

——Become a Great Self-Leader!——

You are born to lead, a queen or king in your own life, able to rule from your center while making conscious, deliberate decisions. Reaching ever-increasing, impassioned self-leadership is your mission and the purpose beneath your goals. When you were born into your life, you developed many assumptions and beliefs about how the world is and how you could or should be in the world. Your destiny is to become consciously aware of where in your life you are not leading from your center. You continuously notice when and how you deal with certain areas of life in a reactive fashion and with a small perspective. You notice where you have challenges, addictions, or other issues. You notice in which aspects of your life you currently believe yourself to be helpless, hopeless, or unable to move forward.

To create a new life requires change, and change requires leadership. Like it or not, you are the leader! Yet, rarely have we learned effective self-leadership skills. While some great leaders are born, most of us have to make a decided, personally directed effort in that direction. Developing effective self-leadership is probably the most important work of your lifetime. Self-leadership is how you influence yourself to define and then take consistent, compassionate action on the dreams that are most important to you. It means that you give meaning and value to your journey, no matter how difficult or long it is. You bring out the best in yourself rather than simply bossing yourself around. You make decisions that allow you to feel more capable and empowered. Strong self-leadership involves everything we have already talked about—determining what you want, setting a course of inspired action, accepting personal responsibility for your actions or lack of action, acknowledging success and effort, following through with your promises to yourself—but also applying humor, grace, and self-loving honesty to your journey.

Being involved in leading yourself through the process of achieving your dreams is not the same as rigidly chasing goals, being a drill sergeant with yourself, or declaring war against your food and body. All too often, individuals attempt the journey of eating differently or weighing differently by attacking their objective with pressure, frustration, anger, or hatred. Being successful requires a different approach. Instead of trying to get rid of something, an effective self-leader puts action into expanding the feelings and outcomes they desire.

Having a goal is a paradox. Looking at it from the outside, you would think that your only purpose is to achieve the goal in whatever way possible, and then your life will be fine. This is quite deceptive. Your goal is much deeper than that. It is filled with, as yet, unrealized potential and self-love. Developing effective self-leadership and creating a new life involves first honoring yourself for the understandings gained from your experiences. Because of those understandings, you now nurture new dreams and learn to move forward with passion, despite encountering a multitude of unforeseeable challenges.

Along your journey lies the great truth of the universe: you can have an idea and, with your own inspired actions, put it into existence! Goals are how you dare yourself to discover if you can create something in your life that does not yet exist. If you march into battle and force your way to your destination, you miss the most amazing mystery of life: you were born with the ability to imagine new life experiences and breathe life into them. You can imagine what a happy life would look like to you and then make it happen. Doing this requires effort, dedication, and persistence. What it does not require is going to war with what you do not want.

No one is forcing you to achieve your goal. It is a free choice made by you, not a prison sentence pronounced upon you. You chose this particular desire because you wanted to experience life in a new way. You are an adventurer! Your journey will help you gain new skills and unleash new aspects of yourself. You will teach yourself entirely new ways of thinking, acting, feeling, and living. Knowing that your outcome is important to you and being able to anchor yourself with an enduring reason for why you want to create change is essential. As you work your way toward your outcome, some days will be wonderfully inspirational and others will be difficult. It takes your big picture vision and your compelling reason to maintain motivation, face challenges, and overcome obstacles. Each step of your journey provides an opportunity to reach deep into yourself and discover your strength, determination, and love.

Being an effective self-leader means learning not to suffer during your journey. Instead, you choose to nurture the positive expectation of your eventual success. You will have what you want, although it is not a function of time. You set a specific goal-outcome date, and this serves to keep you moving forward with a sense of urgency and commitment. In reality, you may not be sure of exactly how or when your desire will manifest, but your timetable keeps you moving forward nonetheless. You refuse to give up until you have what you want. More importantly, you will not punish yourself just because you have not yet mastered the skills necessary to achieve your target. Trust that you will learn. Every difficulty along the way teaches you how to accommodate for a new solution.

The concept of self-leadership represents a personal process through which you positively influence yourself to work toward the successful completion of a specific goal or desire. You take control of your own thoughts and actions to improve your life. Strengthening self-leadership involves:

- building new behaviors, habits, and patterns that increase your enjoyment of life

- attaining confident relationships with life, self, and body

- setting high goals of personal importance

- setting priorities

- shifting focus from the problem to the opportunity

- recognizing and rewarding positive steps toward your desired outcome

- restructuring attitudes and how you think things through

- enlisting creative-problem solving skills for the same old problems

- gaining positive expectations of impending success

- gaining the ability to look into the future and take action today toward that future

- finding meaning in your challenges and purpose in your life

Many personal goals have a tendency to be dismissed before the first month of action passes. One of the reasons is that the goal is set in response to something negative—a habit or situation that the person wants to change or end. While that is a great starting place, there must be more. Pain initiates the journey of change; however, no amount of bullying, nagging, harsh self-discipline, or willful determination will last long enough to carry you to your desired outcome. Achieving a successful and fulfilling outcome requires learning new methods of sustaining motivation and leading yourself. For example:

- How do you treat yourself when you encounter adversity?

- What do you do when your results do not match your expectations?

- Do you deal with challenges utilizing flexibility and creative solution-finding?

- Will you remove your rose-colored glasses and view your situation objectively?

- Will you remove your dark-colored glasses and view you situation com-passionately?

- Will you establish a sense of completion or achievement throughout the journey?

- Are your values reflected in your self-leadership?

Compassionate and effective self-leadership involves the ability to take into consideration your internal resistance and then make decisions that serve your greater objective. Ultimately, you are not a strong self-leader if you fail to abide by your own decisions. For example, imagine that you say you will take a specific action today. Then, you sense a part of you that has resistance. If you end up blindly obeying the resistance you weaken your self-leadership abilities. You have allowed your objection or resistance to lead your life.

It is helpful to recognize that some of your internal aspects are excellent "problem identifiers." That means that certain aspects of you have the wonderful ability to point out potential problems, challenges, and things that could go wrong. These parts of you are adept at recognizing possible difficulties, but it is not their job to assume leadership or come up with a solution. Learn to value your "problem identifiers" for the wisdom they can provide, but do not allow them to take control of your life or stop you from moving forward. Instead, gather the information provided in the objection, understand what it is you do *not* want, bring the potential problems to your creative self, and from there identify new solutions to strengthen your overall plan.

To illustrate this concept, imagine for a moment that you are an elementary school teacher. You are teaching today's lesson plan to a class of twenty eight-year-old students. One of your students, Little Johnny, does not like the direction you are taking and wants to go outside and play instead. Johnny begins to protest and act out. The more you ignore him, the more insistent he becomes. You have several choices. You can silence Johnny and not listen to his complaint. You can punish Johnny for his opposition. You can consider his viewpoint and decide if it has any validity in the larger context. Or, you can give up your leadership position and allow Little Johnny to run the class.

Typically, when we feel anxious, scared, or hear some other internal opposition to moving forward, we allow that part of ourselves to take over. Imagine how silly it would be to give leadership to an eight-year-old while you cower in fear and let him run the class. Just because he was throwing a tantrum and trying to get your attention does not mean that he gets to rule class. Yet, that same scenario is true when you allow your fear or resistance to take over and run your day. Rather than punishing or silencing your "problem identifier" you could stop and listen to the objection. There might just be some valid wisdom contained within the objection. If we retain our heart-based leadership, knowing that we are committed to the overall plan, we can consider the objection and perhaps make some modifications to our actions based on the information obtained.

Strong self-leaders nurture specific characteristics. They learn to be captivated by their vision and take initiative despite internal resistance or conflicting emotions. They accept responsibility for the choices they make. Good self-leaders are not sucked into a victim mentality that blames their problems on their past or other people. Rather, they accept their current limitations and choose to grow beyond them. These people embody optimism, determination, self-discipline, and flexibility. When things are going well, they acknowledge their effort and reward their success. When things are going badly, instead of giving up, they study the situation and adapt their strategy. Strong self-leaders learn to find humor, even in situations that seem difficult.

For example, let us assume that your overall goal states that within ten months you will have a wonderful, new relationship with food, your body, and your life. You will gain the freedom to eat what you want in satisfying amounts. You will enjoy food and eating! That goal is your overall direction; it is what you want most for yourself. In alignment with that goal, you choose an action step for today that states, "After work today, when I normally eat to relieve stress, I will go to the gym as a possible solution." That afternoon, you get home from work with every intention to workout. However, a part of you protests loudly. This aspect of you wants to go eat as it usually does.

That part of you is like Little Johnny. It creates a huge tantrum, insisting that you have to eat to relieve your stress. In the past, you allowed this aspect of you to take over. It was sort of like allowing eight-year-old Johnny to rule the class. That part of you became accustomed to taking over and now insists, quite adamantly, that this is how it has to be. You are not used to leading from your center in this particular area of your life. Therefore, it is going to require will and determination to regain leadership and get all the parts of yourself working as a team toward this new objective.

You have several choices when your internal resistance rises. Just like in the example with Little Johnny, you could silence your resistance and not listen to this complaint. You could punish yourself for being so conflicted. You could consider this alternate viewpoint and decide if it has any validity in the larger context. Or, you could give up in defeat and allow this aspect of you to make the decision to go eat as usual.

Effective leadership requires understanding that you will have internal resistance. However, your objective and compelling core-motivation provide a sense of purpose and direction, creating a tether in the face of challenges. When you are committed to your goal and you know that you are not going to give up your efforts, it becomes safe to consider the viewpoint of the resistance. Why do you want to eat? Is it out of habit? Is this just part of the process that you have to go through to reclaim leadership? Is there a way to listen to the resistance, yet bring it onboard with your new decision to workout? Can you perhaps make a deal with your resistance? Suggest, perhaps that you will workout first, and only *then* if you still feel the overwhelming need to eat will you give-in. Is going to the gym the best way, today, to relieve stress and gain the strength and pride you were looking for?

If you do not yet have strong self-leadership qualities that relate to this particular goal, you may find it hard to move past your resistance. It will be difficult to say "no" to your desire to eat and "yes" to your new course of action. Without cultivating stronger self-leadership as you move through the process of achieving the goal, you will tend to experience or feel the following:

- self-pity

- distrust

- fear instead of confidence, faith, or positive expectation

- worrisome or obsessive over details

- doubtful and undeserving

- impatient for the outcome and discontent with the process

- doubt if the outcome will ever happen

- fear that once the outcome gets here, it will only be lost

- frustration

- fear of imminent failure

- depression

- the desire to find shortcuts, magic cures, and answers outside of yourself

To strengthen your self-leadership skills to move through your eating or weight challenge, it might help to take a close look at some of the other goals you have successfully achieved in the past. You have already achieved many goals in your lifetime. Perhaps it was attaining a college education, making a career shift, learning a new language, writing a sales letter, achieving a promotion, setting a budget, learning a new hobby, or running a successful household or company. The fact that you successfully achieved goals in the past means that you already have the skills, determination, and will to succeed in your current goal.

Out of all the goals you have achieved, concentrate on one goal that you really wanted, that you put effort into attaining, that you enjoyed working toward, and that felt good when you accomplished it. Examine that goal closely and determine exactly how you achieved success. As you focus on that previous goal in which you successfully led yourself to an enjoyable outcome, reflect on these questions:

- What was my first step—how did I get things started?

- How did I keep myself motivated for the long run?

- How did I move through inner resistance?

- How did I maintain optimism and a positive attitude despite challenges?

- How did I speak to myself and cheer myself on?

- What worked best?

- What did not work so well for me?

- How did I feel during the journey?

- How did I feel once I had accomplished my objective?

Take the time to look over your past goal and remember as much information as you can about how you had a dream or a desire. Then reflect on how you made that dream real. Write down those steps below. Then, contrast your past successful strategies with how you typically engage in the goal that concerns your eating or weight challenges. How can you apply the wisdom and knowledge gained from your past successful experiences to your current goal?

_____

_____

_____

_____

_____

_____

_____

_____

_____

Discover Your Self-Leadership Style

Self-leadership characteristics define your behaviors as you work toward your goal. Study the list of character traits in the table below and select the qualities that best characterize you. Circle in **black ink** the character words that best describe your approach to achieving your weight and eating goals. Consider if these character traits positively or negatively affect the quality of your everyday life, the level of your happiness, and the love you have for yourself. Then, go back over the list and circle in **red ink** the character traits that you wish to develop as you approach your goal.

When you are finished, write down your top five **least** empowering self-leadership characteristics:

1. _____

2. _____

3. _____

4. _____

5. _____

Write down the top five self-leadership characteristics that you believe would make your life a more **fulfilled, satisfying, and enjoyable** experience:

1. _____

2. _____

3. _____

4. _____

5. _____

Self-Leadership Character Traits Table

Humble	Courteous	Bored	Inflexible
Brave	Intelligent	Capable	Cold-hearted
Courageous	Honest	Fair	Confident
Serious	Friendly	Doubtful	Fearful
Withdrawn	Adventurous	Gloomy	Joyful
Humorous	Focused	Scared	Cooperative
Sad	Lazy	Wounded	Lovable
Resourceful	Self-pitying	Persistent	Ambitious
Stubborn	Self-reliant	Flexible	Encouraging
Loyal	Bold	Confused	Domineering
Visionary	Harsh	Helpless	Clear
Caring	Daring	Cruel	Curious
Disinterested	Reliable	Discouraged	High-spirited
Dishonest	Cowardly	Compassionate	Decisive
Selfish	Adaptable	Purposeful	Anxious
Unselfish	Fun-loving	Reliable	Inspired
Generous	Successful	Uninvolved	Consistent
Eager	Dependable	Self-disciplined	Determined
Self-confident	Practical	Expectant	Energetic
Respectful	Responsible	Hopeful	Cheerful
Considerate	Complacent	Hopeless	Thoughtful
Imaginative	Fanciful	Considerate	Calm
Tenacious	Happy	Victimized	Balanced
Optimistic	Self-determined	Martyred	Risk-taking
Self-sacrificing	Peaceful	Incorruptible	Hateful
Instinctive	Demanding	Motivated	Rude
Suffering	Sneaky	Willful	Mean
Creative	Bossy	Attentive	Pompous
Experimental	Gentle	Loving	Suspicious
Worried	Aimless	Devoted	Inventive

Increase Your Level of Happiness

Imagine every inch of you humming with life, from the top of your head to the tips of your toes. Visualize yourself energized, excited, and living the life of your dreams. Turning a challenge-filled life into a passion-filled, exciting adventure is possible. However, there is a catch: you have to become accustomed to feeling good. Living your dream is more than just an intangible idea; it encompasses the physical feelings of joy, peace, and competence.

Feeling good is all about the degree to which you feel loved, accepted, and valued—not by others, but by yourself. To achieve this requires learning to refocus your attention away from the problematic and concentrate instead on happiness. You derive these good feelings from being proud of yourself, your efforts, and your accomplishments. Living a life with greater joy is about how you treat yourself when things go right or wrong. Do you acknowledge your effort and success when everything is going smoothly, and do you comfort and soothe yourself when things go wrong? Or, is it just the opposite as you dismiss your efforts and accentuate your failures?

Achieving your goal involves implementing the science of successful goal-setting but that is only half of the picture. You must also activate your spirit. Having successful goals involves creating a new partnership between your spirit self and your physical-life self. To see how this is true, review your compelling reason for setting out on your life-changing adventure. Yes, you want to eat differently, have more control of your life, and be thinner. *Why* is it so important to have what you want? It is for one purpose: to allow yourself to be personally responsible for creating a life that you define as being more joyful.

In one way or another, your compelling reason is about *feeling* better in a human body. Your goal originates from a personal decision to bring more spirit (empowerment, choice, and joy) into union with your physical-life actions. Pursuing this objective means you have taken a step away from hiding out, rebelling, or being angry. Instead of seeing your life as a horrible experience to endure, you have decided to explore other possibilities. You look around and see that happiness *does* exist. Success, healthy eating patterns, positive thinking, and positive results are available. Other people have great relationships with themselves and their bodies. Some have optimal health and boundless energy. So why do you not have those things? Why are you unhappy, unfulfilled, or living with undesired eating behaviors? Is there something different that separates you from someone who has what you want? The answer is, quite simply, "yes." There *is* something different: such people have an ability to identify exactly what they want, focus joyful attention on it, and take inspired and sustained action to attain it.

Always remember, you will only receive in life what you are willing to accept. If you are unhappy then you are willing to accept unhappiness. If you are unfulfilled, then you are willing to accept emptiness. If you are unenergetic or uninspired, then that is what you are willing to accept. That is what is so great about your decision to set a goal! You have decided that you love yourself and you wish to accept a new life experience. You have looked around at life and seen that new possibilities are available. Other people have what you want. Therefore, evidence exists that what you want is obtainable. If others can have it then you can too!

Setting out on a course of self-improvement affirms your desire to live. It is a sign that you want to stop sabotaging yourself, hating your body, clinging to anger, or fearing the physical. Working toward bettering yourself means you are choosing to venture beyond what you think you know and opening yourself to new opportunities. If you keep doing what you have already done then you will keep getting only what you have always gotten. Moving forward is a matter of practicing new behaviors. Shake things up and see if you can bring more of the spiritual into the physical and, as a result, intentionally engage in the act of creating a new experience. The objective of your goal is to let go of old beliefs about what is and is not possible. Your results will not only provide a successful eating or weight result, but also a fresh view of the world as a safe place, filled with abundance and beauty that is available for you to receive.

Setting a goal involves introspection and progressive action. You dream a new existence for yourself and then take the practical and spiritual actions to bring it to fruition. By this process, you intentionally combine physicality with spirit. Your hopes and dreams coalesce with faith and life-energy in a blending of heaven and earth.

You have chosen to focus on a new desire: to discover how the process of deliberate, conscious creation works, to combine your creative spirit with physical action, and eventually to find yourself worthy of receiving your outcome. In the beginning, you probably do not have much, if any, understanding of how to intentionally bring something new to life. You might think it is a matter of luck, working harder, or pushing yourself to make something new happen. The beauty of goals, when approached correctly, is that they teach ways of mastering the unity of spirit with physicality. Goals speak of the love of self, the expansion of new potentials, and of entering into the mystery of who you are. Goals show you how to flow with spirit and with life in a new way.

How do you increase your level of happiness? You have already taken steps to do so when you began to outline your dreams and goals. Your actions amplified your spirit. Perhaps in the past you kept your hopes in a drawer, taking them out occasionally to luxuriate in a fantasy, and then tucking them away again for safekeeping. Yet, each time you decided to take them out of storage, you allowed yourself to consider your wish. It does not matter if you have failed to obtain your goal countless times in the past. What matters is that your dream survives.

Your desires are important and you can decide when you are worthy of realizing them. Dreams are about self-love. They reaffirm the beauty and joy of life. You have set for yourself a difficult task in deciding to end your unwanted eating behaviors and create a new way of living your life, but you will succeed if you persevere. Moreover, you will discover pride in overcoming obstacles. With each positive step you take toward your personally important life direction, your spirit grows. You bring more of your heart into your own life.

Dreams give you the opportunity to feel good right now by allowing you to shift to a sense of curiosity, discovery, and wonderment about what is possible. Consider yourself an immediate winner when you take action on your dream. That's right. You are a success just by entering the arena and participating, regardless of the result. As you follow your creative, inspired actions, your ambitions expand your positive feelings. These feelings are not based on your ability to succeed or fail. They do not have to be earned. On the contrary, as you set a meaningful course for your own life and then take inspired action, you generate happiness.

Feeling good is not dependent on anything other than your decision to receive it or not. It is about embracing a dream, not just having the outcome of a dream. Each day you have the opportunity to make many decisions related to your wish. You can choose to pay attention to what is most important to you. You can move personal priorities to the top of your to-do list. In doing so, your joy will increase as you focus on meaningful pursuits. You can stay on track by asking yourself, "Is the energy I am bringing into my relationship with my dream allowing me to feel good? Are my choices making me feel more empowered? Do my thoughts take me closer to or further from my dream?" If your daily choices, actions, and thoughts move you toward your goal, then you have made decisions that allow you to feel successful and joyful today.

The following three-step process shows an easy way to get in touch with your spirit, to bring the joy of who you are into your physical body, and then connect your joy with your goal. By taking this approach, you can teach yourself a new way of bridging the gap between your spirit and your life. You can feel good as you move beyond your current life experience and step into your newly chosen one. The steps are:

1. Breathe and Center

2. Remember a Moment of Joy

3. "Experience" That Feeling of Success Now

Step 1—Breathe and Center

Most everyone knows, at least on a subconscious awareness level, that taking deep breaths in a tense situation helps manage the emotional response to stressors. Instead of reacting impulsively, breathing creates a physical change, relaxing the body. Breath is the connection between mind, body, and spirit. It brings awareness to physical sensations and anchors us within the moment. It allows us to focus on our desires rather than our fears and automatic responses. Breath opens us to the possibility of allowing creative intelligence to identify solutions that are associated with personal values.

Awareness of breath is a practice that allows you to align the mind, body, and spirit in a powerfully cooperative relationship. In practicing breathing awareness, it is not necessary to make any changes to the physical movement of the breath. There is no need to slow it down, speed it up, or change it in any way. Change occurs naturally as you simply allow yourself to notice.

Close your eyes, take a breath, and ease your awareness into your body. The point is not to achieve perfect relaxation but to notice your breath and your body. Stay with yourself as you become aware of the spirit of breath and physicality of your body. As you inhale *notice* that you are inhaling. As you exhale *notice* that you are exhaling. Breathe and allow acceptance of how things are in this moment to wash over you. After a few breaths, begin noticing the subtlety of breathing.

- Notice the breath entering and exiting your body.
- Notice the quality of your breath: Does it feel jagged or smooth? Does it feel rushed or slow? Does it feel deep or shallow?
- Notice the length of each inhalation and exhalation. Are they even?
- Notice how deeply your breath enters your body. Does it radiate out in all directions with each breath?
- Notice if the body is feeling restricted or tense.
- Notice what happens as you let go of trying to change anything and simply accept.

Continue breathing with awareness until you feel comfortable. You do not have to feel perfectly relaxed or perfect tranquility. Simply breathe until you notice that you have reached greater harmony with yourself. This means that you have reached a place of acceptance without struggle from which you have no desire to flee. Remain sitting and breathing while being aware of your body and the spirit of breath.

Step 2—Remember a Moment of Joy

Continue breathing and remember one instance in life when you had a pleasant feeling. It does not have to be an example of the most joy you have ever had; it could be any experience in your lifetime that felt pleasurable to you. Some examples include cuddling your teddy bear when you were young, walking on a sandy beach while on vacation, or enjoying the unconditional love of your pet.

Place your attention on your breath *and* on this life experience. Recall the stuffed bear, the beach, the puppy, or any enjoyable memory. Take time to visualize the experience fully. See what is important to you in that experience. Make it as realistic as possible. What shade of brown is your bear? What is the color of your pet's fur? How bright is the sandy beach? Can you see yourself in the picture? This is *your* vision, and you get to make it exactly as you wish. Adjust your vision until it is to your liking.

Continue being aware of your breath and your vision, and now bring sound into it. Is there the sound of wind in the palm trees, children laughing with glee, or a happy puppy barking? Are there any voices in your head that speak to you about what a great experience this is? Hear only what you want. If you hear anything that is not to your liking, simply notice, thank the thought for coming, and then move on to another thought. Discover sounds and thoughts that are enjoyable. As you do, bring awareness to your breath and to the sounds in your vision.

Next, add your sense of smell. Not certain what your vision smells like? Make it up! What would you like your vision to smell like? Imagine the scent of the salty sea air, the odor of your puppy's breath, or the smell of your teddy bear's fur. Allow your breath and the smell to commingle within your body.

Finally, bring everything together. This is your own personal, pleasing physical experience. Be cognizant of the feelings in your body. When you bring together the sum of what you see, smell, hear, and even taste, is the overall physical sensation pleasing? Are you warm and alive? Are you more calm, peaceful, or energized? Are you feeling lighter or less burdened? How deeply does your breath enter into your body?

For the sake of making this illustration easier to describe, let us call the feeling flowing through your body "joy." However, the feeling could be anything. It could be warmth, coolness, calm, a tingling of energy, or a release of tension. It could be a feeling of openness or movement. What is important is that you realize this is your physical feeling, you chose to allow this feeling into your body, and decided that it feels enjoyable or pleasurable to you. To simplify things in this explanation, we are calling this feeling joy.

Be aware of your physical body. Notice if your feeling of joy connects with your breath and flows freely through your entire body. Perhaps your feeling flows through some of your body, but not all of it. Notice if your heart is open and accepting to your joy. Be aware of how much joy you allow to flow through your body or how and where you limit this joy. If some part of your body is not allowing the joy to flow through it, then that is okay. There is no right or wrong way to experience joy. Simply notice your body and continue breathing.

If you are not experiencing a positive physical sensation, perhaps you might consider returning to the memorable experience and altering it in a way that will bring about a pleasant feeling. Modify, add, or delete anything that does not make your vision a truly enjoyable experience. As your vision becomes more enjoyable, lightly breathe into your feeling, and allow it to expand. This is sort of like turning up the volume on the television. Breathe tenderly into the feeling and notice if it is possible to gently intensify it.

Step 3—Live Your Success Now

Continue allowing this feeling to flow through your body, even if it does not seem to be "working." Breathe slowly and deeply without force. When you are ready, imagine the situation or life experience you wish to create. This is why you put so much effort into defining your goal: so that you could connect the vision of your success with your joyful, creative spirit.

Remember, your life is both a physical experience and a spiritual one. Setting forth to achieve a goal is the process of bringing your physical self and your spiritual self into balance. Quite often people pray, meditate, or visualize their success but do not involve their physical bodies. They go "off" into a place of peace and possibility and then return into their bodies. What you want is to: 1) discover the peace, joy, and spirit of possibility, 2) bring it into your body, and 3) connect your joy with your physical goals. You do not want your dream to remain a wish or to exist only in the spiritual realm. Rather, your objective is to make your dream become real in this physical reality.

To this end, allow the feeling of joy to continue filling your body and imagine yourself already living your goal. Breathe and notice your feet are on the ground and on earth. Notice how good it feels to connect with your spirit while still being inside your body. Continue engaging all your physical senses to see your success, hear the happiness of your accomplishment, smell your victory, and even taste your achievement. Actively allow the physical experience of joy to unite with your goal. Allow yourself to live and experience your desired life right now, not out in the future.

Use your imagination. There is no right or wrong way to do this exercise. Pretend. Make things up as you put yourself in the picture. Live as you would like to live. Feel that life inside of your body. You can be as energetic, safe, supported, vibrant, and joyful as you want to be. Stand in your body and put yourself in the situation that is satisfying to you. Paint all the details. You get to do whatever you want to do, exactly the way you want to do it, feeling the way you want to about it. Have a conversation. Receive compliments. Adore yourself and be adored.

One of the reasons you began to work on increasing acceptance of your body earlier was so that you could learn to work in partnership with your body to create the life you want to live. In this exercise, you are allowing your dream and your joy to unite within your body. In doing so, you are living your dream. It is momentary but it is real. You are having a physical experience, a trial run, of what you want.

Allow yourself to enjoy this virtual reality as vibrantly as you can. It does not have to be perfect, and this will not be your only chance to form a loving relationship with your desire. Be aware of how easy or difficult it is for you to imagine yourself living this new life. Notice how much joy you allow to run through your body and where you accept or deny it. Observe, as you actively complete this exercise, if you have resistance or if you skip it altogether.

Your ability to feel good is not dependent on the actual achievement of the goal. Happiness or joy is a physical state of being that you may or may not allow yourself to experience. Yes, you want to achieve the outcome of your goal, and that will happen. However, you get to feel good right now. It is only an illusion that you have to achieve an outcome before you can feel good. You do not have to earn joy. By doing this exercise you might notice that the feelings you are looking for do not come from outside. Another person does not give them to you. It is an inner experience prompted by you.

More importantly, the amount of joy you are able to feel now is the exact same level of joy that you would feel at the end of achieving your goal if you did not engage in this exercise. The desire to achieve your goal is really a desire to increase your capacity to experience greater happiness in your body. If you are unable to feel good in your body now, you will not be able to feel good in your body later. The amount of joy that you put into bringing your dream to life is the amount of joy that will be contained in your outcome.

Feeling good is not a concept or mental idea but an active state of allowing your life-energy and spirit-energy to move through your physical body. The sensation of feeling good expands as you learn to connect this energy to your goals and as you utilize this energy to fuel your actions. Merely achieving thinness continues the illusion that happiness comes from outside of yourself or that someone else is responsible for giving it to you. In truth, the feelings you are looking for come from within. They are something that you have control over and can learn to increase.

By participating in this type of visualization exercise often, you are in fact saying yes to the feeling you want to experience. Then, you combine that good feeling with the desired outcome you wish to create. With this combination, you feel dynamic. You increase your passion for living and strengthen new possibilities. The glass is half-full as you notice the sunshine and cheer available. As you focus on your goal with inspiration and desire, you activate the life energy you will need to take daily actions.

The purpose of your goal is to increase your capacity to feel good. To repeat the general steps: 1) Breathe and center. 2) Remember an instance in life when you had the confidence or joy you now seek. See, hear, and feel that experience until it becomes physically real. Breathe in the feeling, and allow yourself to get used to this heightened level of desirable feeling. 3) Connect this feeling with your desired goal outcome. At times, it may be difficult to conjure a reality that you do not yet believe you can have or to see the value of this exercise, but allow yourself to persevere in your efforts. Trust that millions of successful entrepreneurs, business tycoons, winning athletes, and people just like you utilize this ability to focus on a specific desire, connect it to their joyful spirit, and create long-term desirable outcomes. This exercise will open new doors for you also.

What to Do When You Fail

Failure is one of those life experiences most adults would rather not have to face. Yet in actuality, the path to success most often involves experiences of failure. Obstacles and setbacks are an anticipated aspect of any self-improvement journey. Failure is really just feedback telling you when to adjust the plan or to try a new approach. Perhaps the only true failure is when we concede defeat and absolutely give up any effort to expand our life beyond its current state. Failure might also be defined when we harshly criticize ourselves for stumbling, and yet learn nothing from our setbacks. Confucius was attributed as saying, "Our greatest glory is not in never falling but in rising every time we fall." If we embrace our failures along with our successes, learning from each, loving ourselves when we are down, we will grow and achieve more.

A little known formula for success is that success happens because of failure. There are reports that Henry Ford went bankrupt three times before he created a car that worked. Colonel Sanders was sixty-five years old when he first tried to sell his fried chicken recipe. He purportedly took this recipe to over one thousand restaurants before he found a buyer. Walt Disney allegedly spoke with nearly three hundred banks before he was able to attain a loan to start his business. These accounts may be exaggerated, but the point of these stories is that if we can learn to value both our failures and our successes, we will grow and achieve.

The National Weight Control Registry, established in 1994, conducts a research study that seeks to gather information from people who have successfully lost at least thirty pounds and have kept it off for one year or more. They investigate long-term weight-loss maintenance and identify the characteristics of these individuals. They report that everyone who successfully loses weight and maintains this loss has tried and failed previously. Part of their success was due to what they had learned from past failures.

What is the lesson in this? Successful people fail more often than unsuccessful people do. In fact, they fail repeatedly. Successful people do not give up because they have failed. They do not enjoy the experiences of failure any more than you or I, but they view these experiences as learning opportunities. It is important to redefine failure so that you see the experience not as a defeat but simply as "information." From there, it becomes possible to gather insight and include that information in a revised plan.

Even when we understand that failure is expected, failure tends to make us feel bad. This occurs because, not only have we reached a temporary dead end, we connect the experience with judgment and criticism. Additionally, failure triggers and reinforces many limiting beliefs that we already hold about ourselves. Tied to those beliefs are uncomfortable emotions we hope to avoid. It is extremely painful to face the awareness and emotions of helplessness, hopelessness, or perceived weakness.

Some of the self-limiting beliefs activated by an experience of failure include the following:

- I am not good enough to have what I want. (I am unlovable, undeserving, unworthy.)

- I cannot have what I want. (I am different, an outsider, alone, nothing. I should not be alive on earth. I do not belong.)

- I am basically a bad person, and this is the reason for my failure. (I am defective, flawed, imperfect, bad, fat, guilty, a failure. I have poor self-esteem and a sense of being punished.)

- I am powerless to affect change. (I am hopeless, useless, defeated, disempowered. I cannot survive.)

- My needs and desires will never be met. (I am vulnerable, helpless, afraid. I lack security.)

It is impossible to go through the process of achieving your goal without running into all sorts of obstacles, limitations, and setbacks. Part of the reason is inexperience. You neither know how to do what you are trying to do, nor are you supposed to know. Moreover, you have not yet attained faith that your goal is possible. A sense of impending success is something that grows over time with each inspired action you take and complete.

Encountering obstacles, even seemingly insurmountable ones, does not prove you cannot have something. It simply means you have reached the edge of your current abilities.

Not knowing how to do something can threaten self-esteem. This is where expansion of self-love is possible. What do you tell yourself when you face a failure? Do you tell yourself that you are worthy, that you can eventually have what you want, and that you will allow yourself more patience? Will you allow yourself to look compassionately at the failure, gather the wisdom within the experience, and creatively adjust your course of action? If not, this is the opportunity to hone your self-leadership skills and convert challenges into opportunities for personal growth. You can look around, determine what kind of internal and external support you need, and find a way to subscribe to them. Feel what you feel and admit that you do not have all of the answers. Open yourself to discovering greater compassion and determination along the way. These actions demonstrate faith in yourself and faith that you are supported.

Failure is a means to a deeper appreciation and love for your self. You have choices: failure can be utilized as a way to close your heart, or it can be a stepping-stone to new possibilities. You can view failure as evidence of your inherent internal flaws, or you can excavate the internal love, strength, persistence, or faith needed to move through this situation. To set a goal is to practically ensure an encounter with the experience of failure. Failure does not prove that something is wrong with you or that you cannot have what you want. Failure is only a moment in time when you do not yet have what you want.

Failure can guide you toward an awakening of faith. You are capable of overcoming any obstacle, problem, or situation connected with your dream. Why else would you have this particular dream unless it was yours to realize? Failure can teach you to find the light within, especially when the situation appears most bleak. It can teach you to love, encourage, and support yourself through the good times as well as the bad. Love yourself for your willingness to step beyond your comfort zone and for your attempt to create something new, no matter the current outcome.

Learn from the experience. Feel what you must, but do not dwell over the dark feelings too long. As soon as possible, allow the feeling or emotion to continue its energetic movement through you and out of you. Cry if you wish. Express your emotions in writing. Scream at the unfairness of it all. Touch the hard cold wall of your failure. Describe the hopelessness of your situation. Then, when you are ready, go back to the foundation you have so carefully set for yourself. Remember your big picture, remind yourself of your compelling reason for starting on this journey. Remember how excited you felt while defining your goal and imagining potential outcomes. It might take tremendous effort to lift out of the heaviness of failure, but your ability to redirect your attention back to the objective strengthens your self-leadership. You are capable of deciding what you choose to focus on. Your goal was important when you set it, and it remains so.

In the midst of failure, if you examine your feelings objectively, you will find that the impasse derives from a belief that you cannot succeed. As you confront this belief, rely on faith to stay positive. Tell yourself:

I do not want to be feeling and experiencing this failure, but I am. This time, instead of collapsing, I will take time to breathe and become grounded. I am feeling confused and hopeless, and a part of me wants to give up. It is okay that I feel these emotions and think these thoughts, but I do not have to follow that advice. My heart wants me to believe in myself and to continue. I know that I am supported from above and here on earth. I can accomplish my desire without becoming overwhelmed, going crazy, or falling into the depths of depression. I do not know how I am going to move through this obstacle, but I know that I will. I choose to have faith in myself and in my dream. My creative inspiration will guide and direct me by providing new possible solutions. I will begin again.

In addition, now would be a good time to practice the three-step exercise of breathing, remembering a pleasurable experience, and once again connecting your goal with a feeling of success and confidence. Center and revitalize. Treat yourself with compassion and tenderness. No one likes to fail, yet you can move beyond this experience.

Your logic is doing a wonderful job at telling you that you do not have what you want. And that is true for now. You feel badly because you do want your outcome. What you want is important to you and you will continue forward in your quest. To this end, engage your creative inspiration to focus on your overall vision and to provide a doable action step that will once again build confidence. What can you do right now to get back on your horse and begin again? When you have your answer, take that action step.

Failure can provide the opportunity to strengthen your spirit and will. It affords an occasion to choose empowering thoughts, practice reassurance, and reinforce confidence. Make the best of the experience when it occurs. When you experience failure, you can gain insight about yourself and your next move by answering the following questions:

1. What am I experiencing right now?

_____

_____

_____

_____

_____

_____

2. What are my thoughts concerning this experience?

_____

_____

_____

_____

_____

_____

3. What am I feeling?

_____

_____

_____

_____

_____

_____

4. What do I believe about myself and my place in the world as I encounter this dead end?

_____

_____

_____

_____

_____

_____

5. Is this somehow similar to how I felt in certain situations as a child?

_____

_____

_____

_____

_____

_____

6. What does my spirit need to feel safe and trusting?

_____
_____
_____
_____
_____
_____

7. If I were wise and loving, how would I comfort myself? What actions would I take right now to move myself through this experience of failure?

_____
_____
_____
_____
_____
_____

When facing failure, it is acceptable to feel misery and despair. It is understandable to want to give up. At this critical point, you are charged with finding a way to open your heart and comfort yourself. Cry the tears, shout the anger, and bemoan the injustice. It might seem easier to regress into your old habits for finding comfort, particularly because you feel you have reached a dead end. Even so, challenge yourself and ask, "What can I do now?" Although it may be painful, only you can make the choice to have faith and lead yourself forward once again.

Self-Leadership Skills Checklist

Building effective self-leadership is a life-long process of learning to balance intellect with instinct and inspiration. As you begin to see yourself more clearly as a leader, you realize that you are responsible for your own well-being. You accept your current challenges and, in doing so, utilize them to unleash self-determination and stand more solidly in personal core values. Self-leadership is your ability to continuously gain confidence in your self and your ability to focus on your long-term vision. Read the following checklist and note which leadership skills you are currently applying to your goal and which could use more attention. As you pursue your goal, continue to find innovative ways to support yourself, recognize yourself as a worthy person, and celebrate your life!

Planning

_____ I honor my feelings.

_____ I have a clear vision of what is important to me.

_____ I remember my compelling reason.

_____ I will write everything down for at least 21 days.

Decisiveness

_____ Success is a choice.

_____ I know what I want, *and* I know why I want it.

_____ I take daily actions to strengthen my ability to make a choice and follow through.

Mind, Body, Spirit, Balance

_____ I approach my goals with a balance between logic and spirit.

_____ I am respectful to myself.

_____ I am lovable and valuable, and what I want matters to me.

_____ I hold a positive expectation of success.

_____ I nurture loving feelings for my body, my desires, and myself.

_____ I envision my goal accomplished.

_____ I am excited about my goal.

_____ I invoke my creativity to develop potential solutions.

_____ I learn to cheer my own efforts.

Self-Initiative

_____ Success is not a spectator sport—I take daily action.

_____ I take actions that are bold and daring.

_____ I set realistic, achievable goals.

_____ I am willing to experiment with creative solutions.

_____ I feel fear, but I act with bravery.

_____ I am willing to fall down.

_____ I am willing to fail.

_____ I am willing to get back up again.

Personal Responsibility and Commitment

_____ I recognize when a decision needs to be made.

_____ I identify challenges and develop potential solutions.

_____ I assume responsibility for my choices—every choice counts, every choice has a consequence.

_____ I accept that I have control over my world.

_____ I measure my progress.

_____ I reward my progress.

_____ I accept challenges as they arise.

_____ I find value in my failures and learn from them.

_____ I resolve never to give up.

Action

_____ Self-discipline is a habit increased with daily positive action.

_____ I focus my attention.

_____ I prioritize my goals.

_____ I take actions that increase my self-confidence.

_____ I honor my word to myself.

_____ I strengthen and lead with my five chosen self-leadership characteristics.

_____ I set specific targets.

_____ I take daily action.

Joy

_____ I am aware of how my behaviors and attitudes affect my emotional well-being.

_____ I am aware of situations that cause stress, frustration, and emotional upsets.

_____ I develop strategies for reducing stress.

_____ I develop strategies to increase my passion and happiness.

_____ I look for the beauty of life while in the process of accomplishing my goals.

_____ I hold high-expectations for myself.

_____ I create meaning in what I do.

_____ I accentuate the positive.

_____ I look for satisfaction in the small things.

_____ I get absorbed in my activities.

_____ I learn from my failures.

_____ I allow my goals to reveal that my life has meaning and purpose.

A Trip into Your Future

There is a saying that if you have lost your joy, you have lost your spirit. In making the decision to pursue change, you decided to bring more of your spirit into your life. Your goal is the process to accomplish that. However, you cannot expect joy to happen to you. You must generate opportunities that allow you to be more open to the experience of greater joy. Even if you are able to muster only a speck of joy at the outset, that seed, when nurtured, will grow along the way.

Joy can be expressed as the amount of enthusiasm you have for your life and for your goals. Joy could also be called excitement, eagerness, or even passion. Joy is the kind of internal love that says, "Yes! This is a good and important idea. I will spend more time with this idea." As you decide to play with and activate imagined outcomes, you begin to feel good once again, even if it is just a little at first. Even a tiny bit of feeling good makes you gladder to be alive. You will have more energy and ambition to convert into action. Being enthusiastic about your goal will drive you to the best possible outcome. By contrast, if the feelings surrounding your dream are strictly ones of apprehension, fear, or overwhelming pressure, then your goal does not have a chance of developing into the type of outcome you desire. As long as your goal remains bracketed in a negative desire or completely enveloped in a fearful state, the chances of achieving it in the way you want are minuscule.

Vision boards are terrific tools that easily allow excitement to grow. They work by creating a fun and accurate visual representation of your desired outcome. Vision boards help you focus on the particular outcome that is important to you. They help you to see your desire, stimulate your physical senses, and bring life to your goal.

In constructing a vision board, you place images and pictures of what you want to create onto a big sheet of poster board. For example, if your goal is overcoming overeating, creating a happier life, or creating a healthy and fit body, take a little time and ask yourself some meaningful questions:

- What would the dream look like?

- How would life be different if it were truth?

- How would I feel, think, and act if I had what I wanted?

- What strengths would I have, and how would I be using those strengths?

Note what concepts and ideas come to mind. The next step is to put these ideas into the physical world by creating a visual representation. Vision boards help you see the images of your success as if they were already happening. They bridge the world of fantasy and reality. They bring the spirit of your desires into physical form. Furthermore, they help you focus on the direction you are moving. They allow you to expand the excitement necessary to take further actions that bring dreams closer to reality. The key is to find pictures that help you imagine yourself already in possession of your desired outcomes.

Imagination is not simply a visual picture of a wish. It is a full body experience. As you look at your completed vision board, take the time each day to internally create and celebrate this promised new life. Use all of your physical senses, including your sense of love. By combining the elements of sight, smell, sound, taste, and touch to visualize your objective, it becomes tangible. Looking at your vision board helps cultivate a belief of impending success.

To achieve your goal, it is important that you maintain awareness of what you want. You can indeed live the life you want to be living. You can feel good, right now, in this present moment, as you realize you have taken control of your life direction. Life is not something that just happens to you. You are firmly in the driver's seat! Give your vision board your daily attention. By doing so, you remind yourself to focus your energy on your desires. However, just thinking positively about your dreams is not going to make them magically appear. As your motivation and energy increase, listen to your creative ideas, and then direct your efforts toward actions that will generate results.

Create a Vision Board

Change is a today activity. For a dream to come true, every day and every choice matters. However, action means starting at the right place at the right time. Begin by choosing the smallest and most achievable steps that will help you progress toward the desired outcome. Why start so small? First, success builds on success. Second, dramatic, life-changing solutions rarely work. In fact, major changes come as the result of a series of small steps that are taken, completed, acknowledged, and celebrated.

Vision boards are wonderful small steps that leads to momentous results. They are easy and fun to make. All you need are a few simple supplies. In a short amount of time, you will be able to tap into a secret so powerful that it transforms the lives of anyone who discovers it.

1. Purchase a large poster board in whatever color you like. Also, pick up a glue stick and a pair of scissors.

2. Gather an assortment of old magazines, pictures, catalogs, and snapshots.

3. Take some time to create a space where you can relax, spread out, and have fun. Brew a cup of hot tea, light a candle, and put on music that inspires you. Then—this is an important step—breathe deeply, close your eyes, and initiate the three-step process to generate spirit-filled goals: 1) *Breathe and Center*, 2) *Remember a Moment of Joy*, and 3) *Experience That Feeling of Success Now*. Relax, breathe, and find your joy. Connect this feeling with your goal. Take a few minutes and fully envision your dream exactly the way you want to be living it.

4. Now, open your eyes and let the fun continue! Leaf through the magazines and tear out any pictures, images, or phrases that inspire or motivate you. Do not think about it too much. Simply go through the magazines and remove anything that captures your attention. Allow the bulk of your clippings to be pictures and include a few motivational statements that spell out the goals you wish for yourself.

5. Take your time. Give yourself an hour or even an entire evening to create your vision board.

6. When you sense you have all the pictures you need, sort through them and arrange them on your poster. Use the scissors to cut out the words and images that most express your dream. Then glue or paste them on your poster board in whatever arrangement seems most appealing.

7. Have fun doing it! Enjoy yourself! Let your imagination be your guide. You could make this a celebration by inviting several of your closest friends over to join you in the process. Turn on some music, share some food and drink, enjoy laughter, be silly, and enjoy your dream-creating party with those friends or family you most love.

8. Once your board is complete, activate your vision board. Place it in a room or on a wall where you can look at it often for a month or two. Perhaps the best place would be in your office. Alternatively, place it in your bedroom where you can reflect on your goal first thing in the morning and last thing at night. Perhaps it would make an excellent screen saver on your computer monitor. You want to place your vision board in *front* of you so that your desires move from the back of your mind into the forefront. You want to have your goals ahead of you, not sitting *behind* you on the back burner!

Look at your vision board often and allow yourself to experience this "other" life. Use your vision board as a tool to fall in love with the journey. Fall in love with yourself for having a dream. Self-love is a consuming passion for increasing your own happiness. It is a choice to be excited by focusing on meaningful desires and beautiful outcomes. Love is available when you decide that you are important. It is not based on any specific accomplishment. It is not awarded at some magical moment when someone gives permission for you to feel good. Love and joy are available as you connect with your goals, feed yourself with empowering thoughts, and develop in an exciting and sensuous partnership with yourself.

Savor each moment and be deeply appreciative of all that you have. Visualize the abundance of your world. Believe in the inevitability of success. Even if you have no idea how you will accomplish your goal, give it the energy and faith to grow. See your goal through the eyes of love.

As time passes, feel free to add to your board or paste over what does not work. Make it come alive by lingering over it, both when you feel low and when you feel inspired. As you concentrate on these visual images, allow a sense of peace and joy to wash over you. Smile. Concentrate on the sensation of inspiration. Allow your subconscious mind to help you achieve your goals. You now have a self-generated tool that keeps you focused on your desires and allows you to expand your ability to feel good.

Epilogue

—You Are the One You Have Been Waiting For—

Creating a happy life involves believing that you can control your own destiny. To take charge of your own life, you must be able to set goals, evaluate options, make choices, and then utilize positive initiative to reach these goals. This development of self-leadership skills and self-determination is a process that begins in childhood and continues throughout life.

The practice of setting goals in such a structured format as this workbook presents is not the final answer. Instead, this is a step on your journey, a guide of sorts, through which you allow yourself to learn the basic principles involved in consciously and deliberately creating a new life experience. Learning to set goals is a skill that, once mastered, can be used throughout life for effective accomplishment. Goal-setting is a tool designed to show you how to move away from stress, worry, and trying to fix a problem, toward the ability to imagine and expand a new possibility. Effective goal-achieving is how you teach yourself to blend your logic with your creativity, your physicality with your spirit, and through this partnership bring an idea into reality.

Creating a happy life is not tied to reaching an end. Feeling happier requires deciding to live—in a body—and accepting that your physical body feels things, both pleasant and not so pleasant. Life is a sensory experience to be lived, not at some future date, after achieving a future accomplishment or when everything is perfect, but in the moment.

Life can bring with it feelings we believe are negative. As unpleasant as these negative experiences and emotions are, they serve a purpose. You feel the dissatisfaction of current circumstances and this awakens the possibility of a new future. Discontent asks you to stop and consider what is important. Depression can move you toward tremendous spiritual growth. You feel the limits of your love and wonder how much is possible. When you feel the hunger of your life disconnected from authentic passion, you go in search of your fullness. When you feel numb and life loses its magic, you explore more deeply into your own spirit.

Happiness is not a perpetual state of constant blissful emotions. Instead, happiness is having hope and being connected to a worthy purpose. Your goal is your worthy purpose and, through it, you have the ability to create a completely new relationship with yourself and life. This goal of ending emotional eating, compulsive eating, addictive eating, or even bulimia may not sound as glamorous as having a goal to make a million dollars before you are forty, but they are essentially the same. Every goal is an endeavor to move beyond your current definition of what is possible. Every goal is an opportunity to achieve greater worth, love, and peace on the inside and then bring that spirit into connection with your self-chosen, daily actions.

The illusion is that happiness arrives at the end of the goal. In truth, even though you have not yet reached the outcome of your eating and weight goals, it is the responsibility of your journey to expand your capacity to feel desirable feelings every step of the way. Greater happiness lies in your decision to rely gradually less on over-eating coping strategies and to steadily increase attitudes, actions, and abilities that expand your enjoyment of life. These attitudes and abilities include self-awareness, assertiveness, creativity, pride, problem solving, and self-advocacy skills.

In addition, learning to embrace life more fully by savoring the sights, sounds, smells, and tastes of your everyday moments leads to an increased enjoyment of life. For example, you may use food to comfort yourself, but are your actions unconscious ones?

Alternatively, do you allow yourself to take exquisite pleasure in your food? Do you make food choices that appeal to *all* of your senses? Do you listen to your body and once again learn the language of your fullness and satisfaction? Do you give yourself the opportunity to luxuriate in life's wonderful abundance of pleasurable offerings? Consider incorporating the following ideas into your daily life and experimenting with how these new actions can contribute to a sense of fulfillment:

- Get personally involved with your food and cook a meal for yourself twice a week. It is important that your life energy and intentions become a part of the food you prepare and then ingest. We have all heard the expression, "You are what you eat." When you prepare your meals with the positive intentions of your goal, your energy flows into the food. When you eat, the food in turn nourishes your growing intentions.

- Form a partnership with food. Acknowledge the energy in food, inhale and breathe with the life in your food, and accept the energy in food into your own body.

- Share your self-prepared meal with a friend or loved one. Let your friend return the favor and cook for you.

- Make each cooking and eating event a full, delightful, and stimulating sensory experience.

- Choose fruits, vegetables, and whole grains bursting with life! Not because a dietary rule tells you to do so, but because when you want to be more alive, you naturally gravitate toward the foods that carry more life energy.

If you have had enough of overeating, there is a brave, new direction available to you. You have the ability to create a new beginning and to live a joyful, purposeful life. Along the way, though, there is a good chance you will feel emotions that are sometimes intense and painful. You are capable of learning to face and accept these emotions instead of pretending they do not exist. Ultimately, only you can decide if you want to make peace with yourself, your life, and your body. Finding happiness is when you realize that your emotions are your ticket to freedom. They are how you tell yourself to move beyond your current set of beliefs and experiences.

So often, we pray for guidance, hoping that one day we will be rescued from our lives. Without consciously realizing it, we hope that someone, anyone, outside of ourselves will give us what we so desperately need. We wish for a magic solution that will end all our struggles. We expect someone to tell us exactly what to eat and in what proportions. Getting support is wonderful. However, when we reach outside of ourselves for all of our answers and motivation there is a terrible consequence: we do not give ourselves the gift of learning to live in harmony with our physical life or gain a greater understanding of the fact that we are responsible to ourselves for making decisions.

No one, at least in my experience, wakes up one day and suddenly finds him or herself living a rich and fulfilled life. Yet, it is possible for you to have such a life. That satisfied life evolves because you loved yourself and became passionate about the work it would take to build such a life. Your goal of eating peacefully is a worthy goal, yet one filled with plenty of work and toil. You can begrudge your work and look at it as unfair. Alternately, you can realize that your work is the task of increasing your love, life-energy, individuality, joy, and inner peace. While no one wants to go through the difficult emotions and obstacles of change, you can also recognize that nothing in your life is more important than being passionately involved in your own self-chosen goals.

Only you can decide if you are ready to move beyond wishing and hoping into the effort required to create the life you want. Only you can dare to imagine your life being better than you ever thought possible and unleash the love necessary to create such a life. Believe—even if that belief is only a tiny speck of light—that you can have what you want. Believe that your journey is not simply about weight loss or an end to overeating but a glorious adventure through which you will discover your heart once more. Believe that no matter what you encounter along the way, it is through your journey that you will touch your soul.

Everything is potential, and all potentials are yours.

About the Author

Annette Colby, PhD, RD, is an internationally known consultant, educator, and visionary author. Her contagious passion for life is shared in her writing and private practice where she inspires people to believe in themselves and find themselves worthy of achieving their dreams. For over two decades, she has been committed to showing people how to take the pain out of life, turn difficult emotions into joy, release stress, end emotional eating, and move beyond depression into an extraordinary life! Annette lives in Dallas, Texas, with her husband Ray Nowicki and their feline companions Merlin, Solomon, and Ariel.